Fair Use & Copyright Disclosure:

Usage of this book is for personal use or as a guide with your personal work. Reselling or sharing of this book, without the permission of copyright owner, is considered stealing and is prohibited.

If any questions, please contact
info@moenicole.com

Moe Nicole
AUTHOR.CONTENT CURATOR.INTUITIVE

Table of Contents

Introduction	1
Chapter 1: Single Digit Cardinal Numbers	3
Chapter 2: Angel Numbers 10-99	7
Chapter 3: Angel Numbers 100-199	24
Chapter 4: Angel Numbers 200-299	41
Chapter 5: Angel Numbers 300-399	58
Chapter 6: Angel Numbers 400-499	72
Chapter 7: Angel Numbers 500-599	86
Chapter 8: Angel Numbers 600-699	100
Chapter 9: Angel Numbers 700-799	113
Chapter 10: Angel Numbers 800-899	128
Chapter 11: Angel Numbers 900-999	141
Chapter 12: Common 4-Digit Angel Numbers	154
Conclusion	158

INTRODUCTION

Hello, I'm Moe Nicole

Welcome to this space. I'm Moe Nicole, intuitive Divine Feminine & Spiritual Coach. I have an extensive background in Trauma Therapy and use my professional educational background to help others through various stages of their life.

I am a Masters Level Social Worker and Educator in the process of completing my Doctorate in Trauma Studies. Through personal experience and connection to the Divine, I love sharing my gifts with the collective.

Since I was a little girl, I have been fascinated by numbers which lead me to become one of the smartest mathematicians in my graduating class, scoring the highest on my ACT in the school and within the 83rd percentile in the United States! This lead me to become an Algebra teacher where numbers had meaning and life. I can look at a series of numbers and deduce it down to its simplest form within seconds. Now, I teach others how to understand their personal numbers and why certain numbers may follow them on the day to day.

In this Angel Number Guide, I share intuitive messages for Angel Number 0-999 and popular 4-digit universal Angel Numbers from the Divine Feminine Perspective.

I truly believe that Angel Numbers find us at the perfect time, from our Spirit Guides, to share with us messages of hope, guidance, and affirmation as we continue on this journey of life.

- Moe Nicole

Introduction to Angel Numbers

What are Angel Numbers?

Angel numbers have been used within numerology for centuries as a way to relay messages from the spirit world. Everything around us has an energy and carries a message when we encounter it. The presence of Angel Numbers is one of the most prevalent ways to receive messages from the universe. Those who have more of a Divine Connection to the universal law of life are more likely to notice Angel Numbers throughout their life. Angel numbers are a number sequence of usually 2-4 numbers that appear in various places of your life. Some may find them on mailboxes, home addresses, birth dates, time stamps, receipts, license plates, etc. Anywhere numbers can be seen is when you will notice them, when you are open to receive from the spirit world.

Just like living beings, numbers carry an energetic frequency as well. The use of numerology and numbers can be dated back to ancient Kemetic (Egypt's name before the change) times where scribes utilized numbers in their work for the royal ones. Personally, numbers have always guided my life and directions I take, through a personal relationship I have with my spirit guides on this life journey. When I see certain numbers, I know what it means to me in that moment and place. It's used as an affirmation.

How is meaning created from Angel Numbers?

Angel numbers are simply the connection of the various numbers to create meaning. The basic meaning of messages align with the primary number, which is the first number in the sequence and each number after adds to the energy. The primary basic cardinal numbers of numerology are 1-9. All numbers can be deduced down to one of these numbers when simplified. Zero (0), is a magical wild card in the world of numerology and takes on the energy of the numbers around it together.

Are the meanings always the same?

Meanings change depending on when and where you see the Angel Number. For example, seeing 11:11 at work can have a different meaning from seeing it at home before bed. It is all about the context of the moment. Some may find that particular Angel Numbers follow them for much of their life and adopt it as their personal guide. They may use that number as an indicator for what direction to take or for confirmation they are in alignment.

What numbers are included and why?

In this book, I will be sharing with you messages from each angel number ranging from 0-999 from the Divine Feminine Perspective. I do include common 4-digit Angel Numbers in the last chapter of the book that are popular universal numbers. Some people may find that some 4-digit Angel Numbers follow them, such as 1213. This could be seen as Angel Number 121 with 3 being a clarifier. Or, intuitively, you may find that it has been 12 and 13 following you. Either way, with 4 digit numbers, it works just fine to separate the numbers as seen fit, and read for each number.

Chapter 1: Single Digit Cardinal Numbers

Primary basic cardinal numbers range from 0-9. All Angel Numbers can be reduced down to one of these numbers in its simplest form. It is important to know the basic number found in your angel number in order to add clarity to the message for more guidance. Below, I will explain the meanings found within each cardinal number. It is important to note that each number has various meanings and the meanings can change depending on the other number frequencies connected to it. I also share information regarding your Birthday Angel Number that is inherently attached to you when others encounter you along with the years of life that associate with each number.

0: Zero is considered a wild card in the world of numerology. Since it holds no value it can be seen as a placeholder, and energy of magic, or a number that can be easily influenced by others around it.

1: One is a number that carries the frequency of new beginnings and action into something different. It carries the energy of the Sun which has a lot of focus on action, initiation, and a strong connection to self. 1 is a very independent and confident numbers and can stand alone if needed. The energy of number 1 carries an energy of being courageous, bold, and determined. Those who are born on the 1, 10, 19, or 28th of the month carry a primary 1 energy. Years of age that reduce to a 1 represent a 1 energy year of life. For example, ages: 1, 10, 19, 28, 37, 46, 55, and 64.

2: Two is a number that carries the frequency of balance and togetherness. It can represent relationships, scales, and decisions. The number two is one of mediation making decisions, and even legal decisions. It represents the dichotomy of yin and yang, yes and no, day and night, off and on, etc. The moon represents the number 2 in numerology as it handles issues that are not always done in the open or even comfortable. The number 2 is all about finding a way for everything or everyone to win. Those who are born on the 2, 11, 20, or 29th of the month carry a primary 2 energy. Years of age that reduce to a 2 represent a 2 energy year of life. For example, ages: 2, 11, 20, 29, 38, 47, 56, 65, and 74.

3: Three is a number of magic and communication skills. 3 can be a very happy and cheerful number frequency. It deals with your imagination and what can be possible. Anything that deals with communication deals with a 3 energy, such as writing, talking, drawing, or any other artistic endeavor. Jupiter rules the number 3 in the world of numerology because it is all about being expansive through creative and manifestation pursuits. 3 energy is not always patient and can want things to happen when it wants, hence the magic component. Those born on the 3, 12, 21, or 30th of the month carry a primary 3 energy. Years of age that reduce to a 3 represent a 3 energy year of life. For example, ages: 3, 12, 21, 30, 39, 48, 57, 66, 75 and 84.

4: Four is a number of foundations, home, security, stability, and strength. Four represents an energy of reliability for its practicality and trusting energy. Think about the foundation of a home, it's typically built like a square or a rectangle. Not all, but most are. The North Node (In Vedic) and Uranus (Western) rule the number 4 as it relates to doing what needs to be done in order to change or revolutionize something in the world. It's not always easy, but with determination and strong-will, success can be achieved. Those born on the 4, 13, 22, or 31st of the month possess a natural 4 energy. Years of age that reduce to a 4 represent a 4 energy year of life. For example, ages: 4, 13, 22, 31, 40, 49, 58, 67, 76, and 85.

5: Five is a number that represents change, grace, and passion. It represents freedom and adventure. Five is a number of flexibility, and being able to adapt in new situations quickly. Five can carry an energy of novice or child-like freedom and excitement for life. Mercury rules the number 5 as it relates to the potential for illusions. Mercury is a very volatile planet, which means it can change depending on who or what it is around. It doesn't have its own characteristics without the embodiment of others. Those born on the 5, 14, and 23rd were born with a natural 5 energy. Years of age that reduce to a 5 represent a 5 energy year of life. For example, ages: 5, 14, 23, 32, 41, 50, 59, 68, 77 and 86.

6: Six is a number that represents health, organization, responsibility, love, protection, loyalty, teaching, education, and healing within a community and providing service to others. Number six is a big number for truth and righteousness. Venus rules the number 6 as it relates to relationships, love, and what one sees as being valuable. Six energy can also be charming as it wants things to be beautiful and orderly, which relates to Venus energy. Those born on the 6, 15, and 24th of the month are born with a natural 6 energy. Years of age that reduce to a 6 represent a 6 energy year of life. For example, ages: 6, 15, 24, 33, 42, 51, 60, 69, 78, and 87.

7: Seven is a number that represents luck, intelligence, analytical skills, knowledge, wisdom, experience, spirituality and application. Those born with a 7 energy can have a natural instinctual knowledge to them that allows them to connect to various things from a spiritual and analytical perspective. Neptune (Western) and the South Node (Vedic) rules the number 7 as it relates to spirituality, thinking, and doing things that come to you instinctively. Those born on the 7, 16, and 25th of the month possess a natural 7 energy. Years of age that reduce to a 7 represent a 7 energy year of life. For example, ages: 7, 16, 25, 34, 43, 52, 61, 70, 79, and 88.

8: Eight is a number that represents darkness, things that are hidden, manifestations, business, power, success, and realism. 8 energy can come off as very serious as it has a plan and a goal to reach. It can also signify leaving things behind in order to stay focused. This is why Saturn is the ruler of the number 8. Saturn is all about discipline, power, and being the authoritative figure in order to get things done. Every successful business or establishment needs some form of 8 energy in order for its success to be maintained. Those born on the 8, 17, or 26th of the month carry a natural born 8 energy inside of them. Years of age that reduce to an 8 represent an 8 energy year of life. For example, ages: 8, 17, 26, 35, 44, 53, 62, 71, 80, and 89.

9: Nine is a number that represents completion, alchemy, compassion, and daring to do the impossible or unimaginable. Nine can also represent endings as it is the last of the basic cardinal numbers in numerology. Mars is the ruler of the number 9 as it can sometimes appear to be destructive, and sometimes impulsive. Overall, 9 energy has a presidential feel to it, as it is the highest and that can sometimes be looked at like arrogance. Those born on the 9, 18, and 27th of the month carry a natural born 9 energy inside of them. Years of age that reduce to a 9 represent a 9 energy year of life. For example, ages: 9, 18, 27, 36, 45, 54, 63, 72, 81, 90, and 99.

Chapter 2: Angel Numbers 10-99

10: Angel Number 10 carries a frequency of karmic completion of a cycle that is no longer serving you justice. It connects with the 1 and 0 energy, which means something unknown could possibly be affecting your decisions that need to be ended in order to move forward.

11: Angel Number 11 carries a frequency of spirituality, growth, and connection to a higher power. It deduces down to a 2 energy which is all about finding balance with your spirituality, growth, or personal connection with your higher power self.

12: Angel Number 12 carries a frequency of authority that can not be taken from you. It is given. This number deduces to a 3 energy which is all about manifestation and the use of magic. Your words have power and 12 energy is meant to remind you of the power you carry within you.

13: Angel Number 13 carries a frequency of unknown power. It connects the energy of 1 and 3 to bring a 4. Which means there is an action that can be taken to create a new manifestation or creative pursuit in your life that will bring a sense of stability that you have been seeking.

14: Angel Number 14 carries a frequency of personal endurance through quick changes. It connects the energy of 1 and 4 to bring a 5. This can mean an action you take affects your foundation and stability in order to bring about a strong change in your life.

15: Angel Number 15 carries a frequency of making changes within yourself that bring about the structure you need to create and do something new. It connects the energy of 1 and 5 to bring a 6. This can mean an action or your personal confidence increases and brings in more good things.

16: Angel Number 16 carries a frequency of confident direction and order. It connects the energy of 1 and 6 to bring a 7. This can mean that your personal confidence allows you to make room for abundant growth and luck to come your way. You create a more positive attitude to attract more because your spirit guides see it as a way of you allowing them in to help.

17: Angel Number 17 carries a frequency of a burst of good luck from putting yourself in the right places. It connects the energy of a 1 and 7 to bring an 8. This means that your hard work, dedication, and sacrifices are paying off. You are about to receive a reward.

18: Angel Number 18 carries a frequency of self-determination and maturation. It connects the energy of a 1 and 8 to bring a 9. This means that a karmic cycle is coming to an end due to taking responsibility for your life and actions. The more you show that you mean business, the more you grow.

19: Angel Number 19 carries a frequency of coming back to who you are at the core. It connects the energy of a 1 and 9 to bring about another 1. This means that you are ending a cycle of sabotage and walking away from what doesn't serve you, so that you can be authentically you again on your own path.

20: Angel Number 20 carries a frequency of finding balance in the midst of the unknown. It connects the energy of a 2 and 0 to bring about another 2. This means you are being called to create peace in a situation that can turn out of hand if it is not handled in a timely manner. Handle it when you see it.

21: Angel Number 21 carries a frequency of being a part of a connection or collective and allowing yourself to connect. It connects the energy of a 2 and 1 to bring about a 3, which deals with communication. Your connections and communications with others is what allows you to expand your mind and thinking. Do not isolate yourself.

22: *Angel Number 22* carries a frequency of balancing connections and responsibilities. It connects the energy of a 2 and another 2 to bring a 4. You may have a lot going on right now and you are being called to balance everything to where it is manageable or it may be time to release what is not.

23: *Angel Number 23* carries a frequency of communicating with others. It connects the energy of a 2 and 3 to bring a 5. You are being reminded that your communications with others affect the changes in your life. If you don't like what you are experiencing, its ok to say goodbye. What you do frequently becomes your frequency.

24: *Angel Number 24* carries a frequency of finding peace in your home. It connects the energy of a 2 and 4 which brings a 6. You are being called to either give chores, or find new ways to find balance in your home life to where no-one is doing too much.

25: *Angel Number 25* carries a frequency of finding peace in what needs to be done. It connects the energy of a 2 and 5 which brings a 7. You are being called to find peace in whatever changes need to be made in order to gain more knowledge for the future. Its ok to evolve.

26: *Angel Number 26* carries a frequency of connecting with the right people. It connects the energy of a 2 and a 6 to bring an 8. This message is saying a beneficial partnership will bring about success when you are connected with someone who has a similar vision as you.

27: *Angel Number 27* carries a frequency of gaining knowledge from someone else. It connects the energy of a 2 and a 7 to bring a 9. This message is saying that you may be connecting with someone who has some life knowledge and experience that can help you exit a negative or toxic situation you are in. It is wise to heed their messages.

28: Angel Number 28 carries a frequency of utilizing services until you no longer need them. It connects the energy of a 2 and an 8 to bring a 1. This message is saying to use your resources while they are available to you. No one gets anywhere alone and it is ok to utilize the support of other people or other resources in order to reach a personal goal.

29: Angel Number 29 carries a frequency of toxic positivity. It connects the energy of a 2 and a 9 to bring about a 2. This message is saying make sure you are not connecting with people or things that are not allowing you to grow and expand, yet are keeping you stuck in a cycle that is not beneficial for you.

30: Angel Number 30 carries a frequency of unknown communication or direction. It connects the energy of a 3 and 0 to bring about a 3. This message is saying it is important to know that you have alot of options available to you and directions you are able to take in order to succeed. Whatever you do, stay true to yourself and how you get things across and prefer.

31: Angel Number 31 carries a frequency of remembering you are the most important product you will ever nurture. It connects the energy of a 3 and a 1, to bring about a 4. You are being called to always remember that you are the biggest investment you will ever make in life. Whatever you do, always nurture yourself and put your mask on before bending backwards for someone.

32: Angel Number 32 carries a frequency of important conversations. It connects the energy of a 3 and 2 to bring about a 5. You are being called to have difficult conversations in order to bring proper balance for a collective change that needs to be made.

33: Angel Number 33 carries a frequency of random blessings. It connects the energy of a 3 and another 3 to bring about a 6. This number is a reminder that your work and pursuits are bringing random blessings your way that will create the space you need in order to do the things that make your soul feel free. Whatever you are doing, do not stop moving forward.

34: *Angel Number 34* carries a frequency of research and balanced opinions. It connects the energy of a 3 and a 4 to bring about a 7. This angel number is an indicator for you to take some time to research an idea you are bringing to fruition. This new knowledge will be used for years to come. Knowledge is wealth for your endeavors. You may even be called to learn a new language or culture.

35: *Angel Number 35* carries a frequency of allowing your childlike faith to roam free. It connects the energy of a 3 and a 5 to bring about an 8. This angel number is saying it is safe to have a childlike faith and allow your imagination to roam in order to identify the path you'd like to take with work or a business idea. Whatever you do for work, you want to make sure you enjoy it.

36: *Angel Number 36* carries a frequency of organizing your thoughts. It connects the energy of a 3 and a 6 to create a 9. This angel number is saying it is time to organize your thoughts and plans in order to make proper decisions and movement from what is no longer serving you. You can't just wing this idea, you have to be prepared.

37: *Angel Number 37* carries a frequency bettering yourself. It connects the energy of a 3 and a 7 to create a 1. This angel number is saying it is time to take the steps needed to become a better you. Is there something you could be reading, learning, or listening to that will help you with your personal development? No one can take your knowledge from you, that is the greatest wealth you will ever have.

38: *Angel Number 38* carries a frequency of settling an issue. It connects the energy of a 3 and an 8 to create a 2. This angel number is saying it is time to handle an important issue that will bring balance to your life. This could be paying bills, signing documents, or handling conflict management with someone around you in order to have peace and continued movement.

39: Angel Number 39 carries a frequency of self sabotage. It connects the energy of a 3 and a 9 to create a 3. This angel number is reminding you that you have the power to create your reality and sometimes we can self-sabotage communication or opportunities. You are being called to pay attention to your actions, thoughts, and words. Make sure you are not continuing a karmic cycle, yet ending them and starting something new. You have the power to create whatever you want as long as you believe it.

40: Angel Number 40 carries a frequency of "it is what it is." It connects the energy of a 4 and a zero to create a 4. This angel number is reminding you that everything will work out for you, no matter what happens or is happening right now. Keep going and know that you have the power to change the outcome. Your bills, home, stability or whatever else may be bothering you will work out in your favor.

41: Angel Number 41 carries a frequency of finding yourself. It connects the energy of a 4 and a 1 to create a 5. This angel number is here to remind you that it is ok to change, that is a part of life and personal development. As you get older, you learn new things that allow you to change and transform into a new and better version of yourself. You are a compilation of everything you have seen and done; keep going!

42: Angel Number 42 carries a frequency of important connections. It connects the energy of a 4 and a 2 to create a 6. This angel number is here remind you to connect with people who align with your goals and vision. When you are in alignment with your purpose, the right people will appear to help push you further. Healthy relationships are key to growth that keeps you feeling good.

43: Angel Number 43 carries a frequency of deciding a course of action. It connects the energy of a 4 and a 3 to create a 7. This angel number is here to remind you to stand firm in the decisions you make for yourself and personal growth. You are in alignment to create your own luck and what you learn during this time is instrumental for your stability and grounding.

44: Angel Number 44 carries the frequency of stability. It connects the energy of two 4's to create an 8. This angel number is here to inform you that tough times will come to an end soon. You need to make sure that you remain grounded through all things and take things seriously in your life right now. Take care of your responsibilities and stay strong in your personal convictions.

45: Angel Number 45 carries the frequency of changing around the familiar. It connects the energy of a 4 and 5 to create a 9. This angel number is here to recommend that you pay attention to your homelife and the feng shui. You may be wanting to move or redecorate your home. Moving some things around you can bring a different energy and excitement for the completion of a cycle you have moved on from.

46: Angel Number 46 carries the frequency of paying attention to your health and personal needs. It connects the energy of a 4 and 6 which creates a 1. This angel number is calling for you to pay attention to your health and make sure you are making healthy decisions when it comes to your emotional, physical, and spiritual health. You only get one body and you want to make sure you are taking care of it the best you can.

47: Angel Number 47 carries the frequency of understanding your connections. It connects the energy of a 4 and a 7 to create a 2. This angel number is here to remind you to use the knowledge you have gained over the years to make great connections with people. What have you learned about when it comes to communicating and learning how people operate? This is the perfect time to utilize it.

48:Angel Number 48 carries the frequency of handling important matters. It connects the energy of a 4 and an 8 to create a 3. This angel number is here to remind you that it is important to handle important matters that keep a roof over your head, money in your pocket, and entertainment you enjoy. The mundane tasks are important for our survival. You may even have to have a difficult conversation with someone that you have been avoiding.

49: Angel Number 49 carries the frequency of moving on to something different. It connects the energy of a 4 and a 9 to create a 4. This angel number is here to let you know that all things do not last forever. It may be something or someone in your life that you thought would last longer than it is appearing to last now. You are being called to let nature run its course.

50: Angel Number 50 carries the frequency of unpredictability. It connects the energy of a 5 and a 0 to create a 5. This angel number is here to let you know that anything can happen so keep an open mind. Be open to doing something different in order to get different results. You are most likely being called to step out of your comfort zone or just get mentally prepared for a surprise that will shake up your world in a good way. Always remember, perception is everything.

51: Angel Number 51 carries the frequency of self improvement. It connects the energy of a 5 and a 1 to create a 6. This angel number is here to remind you that it is important to change up things sometime in order to stay connected to yourself. You may be called to change a routine, health regiment, or thought process in order to get things on track in your life at the moment.

52: Angel Number 52 carries the frequency of changes in partnerships or connections. It connects the energy of a 5 and a 2 to create a 7. This angel number is here to let you know that changes are coming to your relationships soon as a way to give you experience in a new domain. Whatever you are going through with your partnerships right now, know that it will be working out for your good. You may be called to use your experience from past relationships to aid how you handle your current situations.

53: Angel Number 53 carries the frequency of a change in perception. It connects the energy of a 5 and 3 to create an 8. This angel number is here to let you know that you may want to change your perception about a decision that was made or need to be made. As you change your perception and realize everything is working out for your good, it will make the change flow smoother.

54: Angel Number 54 carries the frequency of being more changing places. It connects the energy of a 5 and 4 to create a 9. This angel number is here to let you know that you may want to consider changing jobs or something else that provides a sense of stability. The time has come when you have outgrown something and it is time to explore what is next.

55: Angel Number 55 carries the frequency of divine protection. It connects the energy of two 5's in order to create a 1. This angel number is here to remind you that you are blessed and highly favored in whatever endeavor you choose to embrace. You have a window of opportunity to start something new and watch it flourish quickly when you put your all into it.

56: Angel Number 56 carries the frequency of a change in roles. It connects the energy of a 5 and a 6 in order to create a 2. This angel number is here to inform you that there may be a change in leadership, ownership, or options due to the decisions of another person. It is best to not get too attached.

57: Angel Number 57 carries the frequency of taking a playful approach to something. It connects the energy of a 5 and a 7 in order to create a 3. This angel number is here to let you know that it is ok to change your approach to a more playful one, when it comes to learning something new. You manifest more lucky moments when you are having fun with what you are doing. Don't take things too seriously.

58: Angel Number 58 carries the frequency of grace. It connects the energy of a 5 and and 8 to create a 4. This angel number is here to let you know that the universe is sending you grace to fix mistakes you have recently made. You are given an opportunity to re-do something in order to have a better outcome for stability and a newfound strength.

59: Angel Number 59 carries the frequency of forced change. It connects the energy of a 5 and a 9 to create a 5. This angel number is here to remind you that you can't plan every ending in your life. Sometimes, things happen that you have no control over. The key is to allow all forced endings to end in order to experience what is coming for you. Everything is working out for your good and you are highly favored through it all.

60: Angel Number 60 carries the frequency of switching a program up. It connects the energy of a 6 and 0 to create a 6. This angel number is here to let you know that at this time in your life it is ok to test out different things as a way to find what works best for you, your schedule, and life in general. What works for one person may not work for you and that is perfectly fine.

61: Angel Number 61 carries the frequency of organizing your personal space. It connects the energy of a 6 and 1 to create a 7. This angel number is here to let you know that it is time to do some research on organizing your personal finances or home needs differently. You may be working harder and not smarter and it is time to make your daily routine simpler in order to free up your energy field to attract more abundance.

62: Angel Number 62 carries the frequency of divine loyalty. It connects the energy of a 6 and a 2 to create an 8. This angel number is here to let you know that you have a loyal partner around you who is committed to building an empire just like you are. You are both teaching each other new ways to do things, such as new structures and processes, that will bring abundance.

63: Angel Number 63 carries the frequency of the end of a dark period. It connects the energy of a 6 and 3 to create a 9. This angel number is here to encourage you to keep going. You or someone else is close to the finish line of something that may have felt daunting or difficult to complete.

64: Angel Number 64 carries the frequency of inter-generational influence. It connects the energy of a 6 and 4 to create a 1. This angel number is here to bring caution to you and your personal understanding of your family history and lineage. As you understand where you came from, it helps you make more informed decisions in the present and future.

65: *Angel Number 65* carries the frequency of changing a routine. It connects the energy of a 6 and 5 to create a 2. This angel number is here, to encourage you to change a relationship dynamic you have with someone or something that does not provide you with a healthy resolution that benefits your growth and development.

66: *Angel Number 66* carries a frequency of health consciousness. It connects the energy of two 6's to create a 3. This angel number is calling for you to look within yourself and address any negative self-talk or behaviors that do not align with your goals. It is asking you to address how you approach and nurture your mental health.

67: *Angel Number 67* carries a frequency of research. It connects the energy of a 6 and 7 to create a 4. This angel number is here to encourage you to research options for support. You may be working on something new or problem solving an issue you are facing. There is support available that will help take a burden off your shoulders in order to keep your stability or other lifestyle aspects.

68: *Angel Number 68* carries a frequency of protecting a characteristic trait. It connects the energy of a 6 and an 8 to create a 5. This angel number appears to alert you that it is important to protect your youthful spirit and no matter what, don't allow the realism of the world to change who you are at the core. Just because you are continuously getting older and maturing doesn't mean you aren't allowed to still have fun.

69: *Angel Number 69* carries a frequency of blocking out energies. It connects the energy of a 6 and a 9 to create a 6. This angel number appears to let you know that you may need to block out an energy from having access to you at this time in your life. There is a cycle that has been completed and in order to get back in alignment with your goals, something has to be removed.

70: Angel Number 70 carries a frequency of unlimited supply and opportunities. It connects the energy of a 7 and a 0 to create a 7. This angel number appears when you need to be reminded that the more knowledge you have, the more opportunities you have available to you to assist you with your goals of expansion.

71: Angel Number 71 carries a frequency of self-improvement. It connects the energy of a 7 and a 1 to create an 8. This angel number shows up in your life when you are at a time of leveling up and advancing to something new, greater, and better. Take advantage of this energy.

72: Angel Number 72 carries a frequency of forward movement with a project. It connects the energy of a 7 and a 2 to create a 9. This angel number shows up to let you know that a period of stagnation is coming to an end. Whether with a project or with a person, you should get prepared for future movement that will end this cycle. It's like out of nowhere, everything falls in alignment.

73: Angel Number 73 carries a frequency of speaking things into existence. It connects the energy of a 7 and a 3 to create a 1. This angel number shows up to remind you that you are able to speak anything you want into existence by not only believing but putting your knowledge into play as well.

74: Angel Number 74 carries a frequency of new contracts. It connects the energy of a 7 and a 4 to create a 2. This angel number shows up to inform you about new opportunities that will be appearing around you. You will be forced to apply knowledge you have learned in the past in order to make great judgment in future endeavors.

75: Angel Number 75 carries a frequency of increased intuition. It connects the energy of a 7 and a 5 to create a 3. This angel number appears when you are being called to use your intuition more when it comes to making decisions, especially when it relates to your spiritual self. You may have been thinking more logically than you should, which has affected your ability to manifest.

76: Angel Number 76 carries a frequency of intentionality. It connects the energy of a 7 and a 6 to create a 4. This angel number shows up when your guides want you to be intentional with your actions and personal schedule. If you are not intentional at this time, you run the risk of losing valuable time and energy when something could've been completed sooner.

77: Angel Number 77 carries a frequency of a change of luck. It connects the energy of two 7's to create a 5. This angel number appears when your guides want to warn you about a swift change of luck that is coming your way. It's ok to get excited, you deserve this!

78: Angel Number 78 carries a frequency of calculated risks. It connects the energy of a 7 and 8 to create a 6. This angel number is appearing to tell you the importance of taking calculated risks for future gain that will benefit generations to come after you. You are in a space of preparation and order.

79: Angel Number 79 carries a frequency of graduation. It connects the energy of a 7 and 9 to create a 7. This angel number is appearing in your life when you are being called to graduate from one way of thinking or being into a new way of life or train of thought. You have matured and are ready to receive more at the next level of life.

80: Angel Number 80 carries a frequency of unknown territory. It connects the energy of an 8 and 0 to create an 8. This angel number is here to warn you that you are walking into unknown territory so make sure you are on your p's and q's. Anything is bound to happen so if you stay ready you won't have to worry about getting ready.

81: Angel Number 81 carries a frequency of outdated methods. It connects the energy of an 8 and 1 to create a 9. This angel number appears when you are being called to take a new approach towards your work or business endeavors. It is time to find a new way to address your situation and make sure to keep an air of realism surrounding you at this moment.

82: Angel Number 82 carries a frequency of privacy. It connects the energy of an 8 and 2 to create a 1. This angel number is here to remind you that everything does not need to be shared with the world, especially if you are starting something new at this time in your life. It is important that you work silently until all matters are settled and secured.

83: Angel Number 83 carries a frequency of important conversations. It connects the energy of an 8 and 3 to create a 2. This angel number appears when you are being called to schedule important meetings and dealings to help you manifest your current goals. There is opportunity ahead for you, just make sure you are confident in your speech and what you have to offer in the new situation.

84: Angel Number 84 carries a frequency of intentional locations. It connects the energy of an 8 and 4 to create a 3. This angel number is here to encourage you to move with intention. Even down to how you decorate and maintain your home, business location, and your car. At this time, nothing should be up to chance; it's ok to control the direction of things in your life right now to ensure order and success.

85: Angel Number 85 carries a frequency of change in leadership. It connects the energy of an 8 and 5 to create a 4. This angel number is either warning or letting you know that it is time for a new leader in an area of your life or surroundings. Someone is no longer able to fulfill the duties of their position and it's time to find someone new who is able to push things forward.

86: Angel Number 86 carries a frequency of new standards. It connects the energy of an 8 and 6 to create a 5. This angel number appears when it is time to raise your standards in an area of your life. You may have been playing it safe and you are being called to increase your standards if you are ready to attract more. You will attract what you feel you deserve and how you present yourself to the world.

87: Angel Number 87 carries a frequency of unrecognizable gifts and blessings. It connects the energy of an 8 and 7 to create a 6. This angel number is here to let you know that you have natural gifts that will help you get through an unknown situation. You will naturally be able to do it as if you had studied for years. It is instinctively inside of you.

88: Angel Number 88 carries a frequency of manifesting greatness. It connects the energy of two 8's to create a 7. This angel number appears to inform you that you are in the process of manifesting greatness in your life. Anything you want is available to you as long as you believe and take the steps necessary to achieve. Let go of any boundaries holding you back.

89: Angel Number 89 carries a frequency of divine endings. It connects the energy of an 8 and 9 to create an 8. This angel number is here to let you know that all endings are a part of a bigger plan. Allow it to happen and go with the flow. You have outgrown something and you are being called to walk into an unknown energy.

90: Angel Number 90 carries a frequency of new beginnings. It connects the energy of a 9 and 0 to create a 9. This angel number appears when you have completed a cycle and are being called to walk into the unknown with no fear. You will be supported in whatever endeavor you choose to embrace.

91: Angel Number 91 carries a frequency of personal growth. It connects the energy of a 9 and 1 to create a 1. This angel number is here to remind you that it is important to embrace endings and go after what makes you feel free and confident in yourself.

92: Angel Number 92 carries a frequency of compassion. It connects the energy of a 9 and 2 to create a 2. This angel number appears when you are being called to be more compassionate to those around you. You are being called to see a situation from another perspective in order to find balance between both opinions or personal desires. Peace and Harmony is important at this time.

93: Angel Number 93 carries a frequency of new communication. It connects the energy of a 9 and 3 to create a 3. This angel number appears when a new line of communication is being called for. You are being called to present yourself or communicate your desires in a new and creative way to where it will be received as how you intend. There may be a current disconnect between your message and the receptiveness of it.

94: Angel Number 94 carries a frequency of increased space. It connects the energy of a 9 and 4 to create a 4. This angel number appears when you are in a space that no longer suites your needs or privacy. You may be looking for a bigger home, new bank account, or car for example. Whatever it is, you have outgrown something that is a need and it's time to expand your territory.

95: Angel Number 95 carries a frequency of gambling. It connects the energy of a 9 and a 5 to create a 5. This angel number appears when the universe wants you to take a gamble on yourself or something else. Whatever you do, do not allow fear to stop you from taking a chance that has the potential to change your life!

96: Angel Number 96 carries a frequency of change in health. It connects the energy of a 9 and a 6 to create a 6. This angel number appears when you are being called to be more gentle on your body and with what you put in your body. As you get older you may not be able to do some of the things you did when you were younger. You want to make sure you are always allowing your body to get stronger to remain healthy.

97: Angel Number 97 carries a frequency of a change in status. It connects the energy of a 9 and a 7 to create a 7. This angel number is here to inform you that you are evolving into a wise being and will be sought after for advice and guidance. You have experienced a lot in life and it is time to share that wisdom and knowledge with others.

98: Angel Number 98 carries a frequency of promotion. It connects the energy of a 9 and an 8 to create an 8. This angel number is here to reward you for the growth and dedication that you have been putting forth. You are going through an initiation and promotion either spiritually or physically. Be prepared for more responsibilities and access to the unknown.

99: Angel Number 99 carries a frequency of evolution. It connects the energy of two 9's to keep the 9 energy. This angel number is here to let you know that it is time to bloom and evolve into something new. You have completed an assignment and are being rewarded and reminded that you are in the energy of creating anything you desire as long as you believe and put forth the effort.

Chapter 3: Angel Numbers 100-199

100: Angel Number 100 reveals itself when you are ready to explore the unknown world. The less expectations you have right now, the more beneficial it will be for your various pursuits. Anything is possible at this time and it is important that you do not limit yourself. Anything is possible right now.

101: Angel Number 101 reveals itself when your guides want you to do something unpredictable in order to benefit yourself and your personal growth. You may have been doing things too much by the book and it is time to switch it up and do something unexpected. It's time to confuse the opps.

102: Angel Number 102 reveals itself when your guides want you to be open to possibilities in new partnerships and deals. It is important to not have a specific goal in mind because it can negatively affect your relationships right now. Allow yourself to have an open mind and be open to other perceptions.

103: Angel Number 103 reveals itself when your guides want you to try something different from what you have done before. Change up how you speak, learn a new language, or just pay attention to how you perceive the world around you. You can create new stability by changing your appearance or creative pursuits.

104: Angel Number 104 reveals itself when you are being called to look at the opportunities for change that are already present in your energetic field. You have the ability to change your circumstances by making a simple change to your current environment. Location is everything. If you are having a hard time with productivity, try working from a new location.

105: *Angel Number 105* reveals itself when you need a reminder that you are the master of your life. It is time to take control of your surroundings and not just let life pass you by. When you make these important changes you will feel a new sense of freedom and structure to be more productive

106: *Angel Number 106* appears when you are being called to get more structured in your day to day life. If you are on the search for knowledge, growth, or increase; it is important that you have the proper structures in place to allow for it to flow into your life from a higher spiritual plane.

107: *Angel Number 107* is here to remind you that your spiritual practices are imperative for you and your personal growth. You are being called to learn more about who you are spiritually and how to embed it into your daily life, especially if it has been feeling like life has been going out of control lately.

108: *Angel Number 108* appears when you are preparing to enter a new phase of your life. You have walked into your power recently and are being prepared for elevation as your current space is no longer able to provide you with what is needed to keep evolving. Growth and expansion is good for you right now.

109: *Angel Number 109* is here to remind you that life is a continuous journey. As soon as you feel like you have everything figured out, you are being called to walk into new uncharted territory. The more you treat life like an adventure the easier it becomes to navigate.

110: *Angel Number 110* is here to let you know that you have the power to fulfill your own destiny by connecting with yourself and valuable resources. You are being reminded that you have unlimited potential already inside of you, just make sure you keep your mind and spirit self in alignment with each other.

111: **Angel Number 111** appears when you need a reminder to pay attention to how you communicate with yourself and about yourself. As you become aware of your personal ways of self sabotaging, it helps you stay in alignment. 111 appears when you need to make sure your spiritual, physical, and mental health are in alignment with each other.

112: **Angel Number 112** appears when you are being called to take action towards a new endeavor or relationship that brings promise of a secure foundation. You are being called to trust yourself and your ability to have a good judge of character and respect for others at the same time.

113: **Angel Number 113** appears when your spirit guides want you to take action towards a new creative pursuit. It is time to change some things in your immediate life in order to keep the excitement going, especially if you have been feeling bored with everything. By starting this new creative project you will find yourself enjoying day to day tasks to a greater extent.

114: **Angel Number 114** appears when you need to take a personal assessment of your current surroundings. How is your home life? Work Life? Daily Schedule? Your spirit guides are calling for you to do some rearranging in order to attract more stability and financial wealth. By taking this action you are able to set boundaries that are harder to be crossed by others.

115: **Angel Number 115** appears in your life when you are taking needed action to change the flow of your life. You are being called to make room for more abundance by addressing your personal fears and changing your approach to life and things that are different from your normal way of being. This will bring more clarity and information your way to increase your self-awareness and knowledge.

116: **Angel Number 116** appears when you are being called to take back control of your spiritual health. You may have been engaging in behaviors that went against the growth you have been making and your guides want you to set some boundaries for the time being, until you are strong enough to not be influenced by old behaviors or people from your past.

117: Angel Number 117 is here to let you know that you are gaining more knowledge about yourself spiritually and it is improving your relationship with your spirit guides. This is bringing about a stronger intuition and your spirit guides want to let you know that it is ok to trust your intuitive nudges at this time. They are guiding you to end something in order to walk towards a new beginning.

118: Angel Number 118 appears when you need to be reminded of how far you've come with your spiritual growth. You have taken responsibility for your life and it is important that you don't allow the opinions of others to change your perception of growth. Keep leading your life into the direction of your purpose, you are in alignment with your higher self.

119: Angel Number 119 shows up in your energy when your spirit guides want you to have more compassion for someone around you. They are going through a spiritual change and need someone who won't judge them for their personal process. It doesn't mean you are supposed to carry them, it just means they need your compassion during this time of their life. Keep them lifted in good energy from the background.

120: Angel Number 120 shows up when your spirit guides want you to use your spiritual authority to return anything that is meant to harm you (or hurt you) back to the sender. If you have been feeling anything mimicking depression or intense sadness, this is a reminder that you have the power to command those energies away from you. Cast it away from you and go outside in nature to allow yourself to be refilled with good energy.

121: Angel Number 121 shows up when your guides want you to remember that you have an important job to do in this lifetime. You have more of an effect on others than you may know and you are being called to walk more in your purpose with confidence and grounding. It is important for you to know that you impact your surroundings, just don't let your surrounding impact you and your mood.

122: Angel Number 122 brings a message from your spirit guides that it is time to take a leap of faith with a new partnership. By connecting with the right people around you, you will then be introduced to new ideas and opportunities that wouldn't have been possible without the connection.

***123:** Angel Number 123* is here to encourage you and remind you that everything is working out for your good and divine order. The actions you take today have a profound effect on your mental and spiritual health as you continue forward. Stay in alignment and keep a positive mindset through it all.

***124:** Angel Number 124* appears when you are being called to take a look at your current alliances. You are only as strong as the weakest link in your village so make sure whoever is around you is aligned with purpose and you share common interests and goals. When you are in abundant energy but surrounding yourself with people in a lack energy, that can rub off on you and your productivity and ability to manifest.

***125:** Angel Number 125* appears when your spirit guides are calling for you to move with intention and to make sure that any changes you make right now in your life are aligned with your overall goal. People are watching you and it is important for you to keep your self respect because someone may be waiting for you to make a mistake in order to take your position of power or leadership.

***126:** Angel Number 126* appears when you are in need to balance your personal needs and wants with what is best for you in the long run. This may not be the time to take a major risk in your life as it may bring a quick ending that you weren't prepared for. Instead, plan your course of action so you can be prepared for what may happen.

***127:** Angel Number 127* is a message from your spirit guides to balance your knowledge and intuition so they can coexist together. You may be using one more than the other and your guides want you to find a way to allow them both to work together. It is important to know when you should use your analytical skills and when you should move out of instinct. Mental Health balance is key.

***128:** Angel Number 128* appears when your spirit guides want to remind you that you are not alone and that you don't have to do everything alone. You have people on earth and in the heavens who are ready to come to your aid, all you have to do is ask for their support. It's ok to let others help you in situations you are not well versed in working through.

129: Angel Number 129 shows up when you are being called to reassess how you communicate endings with others. It is important to leave situations with good karma. If you need to end a situation that is no longer working for you, try to find empathy and understanding in how you choose to do it. Not everyone deserves to be ghosted. Make sure you aren't mishandling any connections around you.

130: Angel Number 130 appears when your spirit guides want to remind you that your words have power. You have the power to build someone up with confidence and you also have the power to tear them down. People listen to you and are watching how you operate; stay attentive.

131: Angel Number 131 shows up when your spirit guides want you to know that you are very magical and are a powerful manifester. You have the power to speak things into existence. When you say you are going to do something, you find success when you put your all into it. It is time for you to use your creativity to change your life around into what you crave the most.

132: Angel Number 132 brings a message from your spirit team to allow your creativity to connect you with new people and collaborations. You may feel like you need some excitement in your life at this time. Do more of what makes you feel good and then seen various doors be opened for you, on top of more order in your life.

133: Angel Number 133 brings a message of remembering that you are the main character and co-creator of your life. Allow yourself to connect with your creative side, speak life into your visions and goals, and watch it all begin to unfold in your life in due time. Whatever you do, make sure you research new ideas before jumping into them.

134: Angel number 134 is a message from your guides to allow time for things to transpire. You may have recently started something new and are finding yourself worrying about how long it is taking to manifest. Spirit wants you to remember that things happen in its own timing at the perfect time. Use this time to speak with your guides and ask them what you could be doing during this time to prepare for the manifestations that are enroute to you.

135: Angel Number 135 is a message of taking accountability for your current situations that you do not like. There are some changes that need to be made in either the area of communication with others, self-talk, or how you view change in general. Pessimism is an enemy to optimism. It's important to be self aware because you want to manifest more of what you want and not more of what you don't want.

136: Angel Number 136 appears when your spirit guides want you to find a creative way to handle your current responsibilities and needs. For example if you have been feeling called to work out more, but the idea of it gives you anxiety, maybe you can try zumba which adds the fun aspect of dancing to working out. There is alway a way around the mundane tasks we don't like to do. Find a way to make them more enjoyable.

137: Angel Number 137 appears when you are being called to document something important that will be helpful for others in the future. You may feel the urge to write a book or document a process you follow. Whatever it is, your spirit guides want you to create something that will outlive your physical presence in the world.

138: Angel Number 138 appears when your spirit guides want you to embrace more of your differences. You may have been wanting to fit into a space that you don't belong to. This is the perfect time to take control of your life and create a safe space for you to allow your soul and spirit to be free.

139: Angel Number 139 appears when your guides are asking for you to end something that is no longer suitable for you and where you are headed. You are creating new things in your life and as you elevate every old habit or person can't go along. Allow yourself to align with your spirit self to see what needs to end in order for you to stay on track with what you are currently manifesting.

140: Angel Number 140 appears when it is time for you to take inventory of your current living situation. Is it still a good fit for you or is it time to start looking to move or switch cities? This is a reminder for you to make sure you are planted in a space where you are able to bloom into your best self.

141: Angel Number 141 brings a message of comfort when you see it. It is your spirit guides letting you know that you are divinely protected and that everything you are doing is in alignment with the goals and plans that you have set for yourself. Keep doing what you are doing.

142: Angel Number 142 shows in your life when you are being called to see how you can balance all of your responsibilities easily. You may have alot on your plate and alot of people who you communicate with on the daily basis. This angel number is a message from your guides to make sure you are staying grounded in your communications, plans, and how you approach your connections with others.

143: Angel Number 143 brings a message from your spirit guides to remind you that it is ok to dream and keep a childlike faith during your day to day routines. When it comes to manifesting, how we speak about ourselves and life have a profound effect on the outcomes we manifest. This is a reminder to speak good to yourself and about your life right now. If you aren't happy with what you have now, you won't be happy when you receive more.

144: Angel Number 144 is letting you know that it is time to get a little serious about something in your life right now. Something or someone needs your attention and its imperative that you show up with an open spirit and compassion. You have the power to help move something or someone in a forward direction by being grounded.

145: Angel Number 145 appears when you are embracing the new changes in your life that affect your home and stability. Open your eyes, there are opportunities all around you and it is best for you to take advantage of every last one because it would do you much justice and good in the long run.

146: Angel Number 146 brings a message from your guides to understand where you fit in, in the settings around you. It's important to read the room when you enter spaces to see how you can benefit a space and how the space can benefit you as well. By being attentive in this way, you are able to see more opportunities around you with connections and collaborations that were meant for you.

147: Angel Number 147 appears when you are being called to research something new that will affect your home life, money, and stability. You may be able to find lower interest rates during this time for example. Whatever it is, spirit is calling for you to get creative with finding new ways to do something. You will eventually feel like a guru in this area over time.

148: Angel Number 148 appears when you are called to move in more silence and secrecy. This is a period where you do not want to reveal too much information before the proper time because random wrenches may be thrown in your plans. Especially, if you have been feeling like someone around you does not want you to experience good things. Solidify the plan, then share it with others.

149: Angel Number 149 appears when your spirit guides want to draw your attention to a change that needs to be made in your home life. Something is outdated and it is time to embrace something new in order to bring it back to life.

150: Angel Number 150 appears when your spirit guides want to warn you about confusing times that are either happening now or are about to happen. They want you to know that although life may feel like a daily wildcard, it is simply shaking your environment up to get the weak links and negative energies out of your space. Stay positive and hopeful during these transitions.

151: Angel Number 151 appears when your spirit guides are calling for you to make an important informed decision in your life at this time. The changes will be a major benefit for you and your learning experience as you prepare to walk into a new season of your life. These new beginnings will change your life for the better as you will gain information and knowledge that is priceless.

152: Angel Number 152 shows itself when you are in a place where it may be hard to see a light. During your difficult times, it's ok to lean on the support of a loved one to help you see a different perspective in the situation you are currently in. This union will give you the strength you need to keep moving forward.

153: Angel Number 153 appears after you are introduced to a new way of doing something in your life. Your spirit guides are calling for you to incorporate this new skill into your daily activities or a new project you are being called to partake in.

154: Angel Number 154 appears when you go through a dramatic change in your stability, home, or finances. It is calling for you to remain open-minded and know that with changes sometimes it takes a while for you to see the benefits of the changes.

155: Angel Number 155 sends a message of having grace for yourself as you go through a transition in your life currently. Your guides want you to connect with the journey and allow yourself to make mistakes in order to master your craft or new situation. You are in alignment and everything is going to be back balanced sooner than you think. Keep going!

156: Angel Number 156 appears when your spirit guides are calling for you to make an important change in how you manage your finances and spending. You may be making reckless decisions that can potentially affect something you will need to purchase soon. Make sure you have something set to the side in your savings account for rainy days.

157: Angel Number 157 sends a message from your spirit guides to go out and learn something new that can benefit your work life and make you more marketable. It may be a good idea to look into a new conference, course program, or something else that teaches you something new that can be utilized in your work field.

158: Angel Number 158 appears when your spirit guides are calling for you to take charge of your life and create the life you have been desiring to live. If you have been waiting for opportunities to happen for you, your spirit guides want you to create the opportunities for yourself. You are stronger and smarter than you think! Use your resources and strong-will to make it happen.

159: Angel Number 159 shows up when your spirit guides want you to take a leap of faith and leave something behind that is no longer serving you. It will seem as soon as you make the random changes everything seems to fall into place automatically like it was destined to happen.

160: Angel Number 160 appears when your spirit guides want you to put yourself first more. You may have been giving a lot of yourself to others and not taking time for your personal needs. You are being called to schedule yourself a day out where you date yourself. You can schedule the beginning of the day and let the rest of the day flow and see what happens.

161: Angel Number 161 shows up when your spirit guides want you to know that you have more influence over your life than you may realize. If it has been feeling like you don't have much control, your guides want you to take a step back and gain control over your life and those who you allow in. You may need to create stronger boundaries and say no more often.

162: Angel Number 162 appears when your spirit guides want you to work with someone else to create a schedule that you both can be held accountable to. There is something you are not meant to do alone, but with another person. You are at the end of a season where you will be feeling like there is no support. It's ok to work with someone else on a project.

163: Angel Number 163 appears when your guides are wanting you to make sure you are communicating your needs and boundaries clearly with your co-workers, loved ones, and others who may be crossing your comfort zone

164: Angel Number 164 shows up when your spirit guides want you to pay more attention to your spiritual needs and growth. It is time to do some grounding activities to make sure you remain aligned with your spirit and physical self, especially in tough times.

165: Angel Number 165 appears when your spirit guides want to get your attention and pass an important message to you. There is an ancestor who has crossed over who has a piece of information they have been trying to share in your dreams. Make sure you are getting enough sleep at night.

166: Angel Number 166 appears when your spirit guides are calling for you to take some time out of your schedule and help someone else with something in their life. It may even be a great idea to find a community to volunteer as a way to give back. You will find great joy in giving your time cheerfully to others who want your help.

167: Angel Number 167 carries the message of needing to get your responsibilities in order. You are being called to research alternative methods for health issues. A current treatment may not be working how it was expected, leading you to seek alternative methods.

168: Angel Number 168 appears when your spirit guides want you to start planning out an idea that has been given to you. You have the strength and strong-will to bring it to life, just make sure you get all of the planning in order to ensure its success.

169: Angel Number 169 shows itself when you are at the end of a cycle that you have been preparing for. Your spirit guides are preparing you for a new journey that will bring a new found excitement for learning and life.

170: Angel Number 170 appears when your spirit guides want you to look at how far you have come. You have learned a lot over the years and it is important to take a moment and acknowledge how protected and divine you are. Anything could've happened, but you are here in this moment thriving more than you may be realizing.

171: Angel Number 171 appears when your spirit guides want you to learn more about something before moving forward. You are in the middle of a transition or transformation of some sort and they want you to make sure you have all of the important information needed in order to make the most informed decision.

***172:** Angel Number 172* appears when you are being called to take notice of the current karma you are creating. What you are creating today will have an impact on the next year ahead so make sure you are giving the same energy you'd like to receive back.

***173:** Angel Number 173* shows itself when your guides are calling for you to address conversations that you may have been trying to avoid. By having those uncomfortable conversations you will open the door for a situation to reach resolution. This is a message telling you that you are the one who has to initiate it.

***174:** Angel Number 174* appears when your guides are asking for you to use your historical knowledge about something in order to guide a decision you need to make. You have the wisdom already inside of you and there is no need to seek outside of you.

***175:** Angel Number 175* appears when you are ready to take what you have learned and go a step further in an area of your life. You have the energy of your guides pushing you to be successful. All you have to do is take the first step and everything will balance itself out naturally.

***176:** Angel Number 176* appears to call your attention to a habit you have had for quite some time. It is important to take an assessment of if that habit has had a positive or negative impact on your life. Then make adjustments accordingly.

***177:** Angel Number 177* is here to bring a message from your spirit team that you are preparing to walk into a lucky time of your life. Whatever you do, make sure you do not allow too many people access into your inner world and thoughts as you work on something new.

***178:** Angel Number 178* appears when your spirit team is working hard to get your attention to an important detail in front of you. Someone may be being sneaky and you haven't been allowing our intuition to share with you what it is picking up. You are being asked to pay attention to your body's reactions when you are around certain people.

179: Angel Number 179 appears when your spirit team wants you to make an educated decision. You are being asked to use your wisdom to help decide a path to take when it comes to your work life and what you are putting your time and energy towards. If you are not receiving reciprocity it is time to take a look at if you are limiting yourself by not addressing an issue. Collect your data and facts to help with addressing it.

180: Angel Number 180 shows up when your spirit guides are calling for you to make an executive decision and follow the path you feel is best for you. Others may not like it, but you know what is best for you and what isn't. Trust yourself.

181: Angel Number 181 appears when your spirit guides want to remind you that you have come a long way and the life you are living right now is the manifestation of actions you have taken in the past. Always remember you have the power to make anything happen as long as you put the work in to do it.

182: Angel Number 182 appears when you are being called to connect with another person to bring a goal into fruition. You are a powerful manifester, but your guides want you to see how you can multiply your strength by connecting with other powerful manifesters. There is someone already around you that your guides want you to connect with. Use your intuition.

183: Angel Number 183 shows up when your guides are nudging you to speak up. Where are you holding back your voice? This is where they would like for you to speak more of your personal truth. Others will appreciate hearing your truth more than you may realize.

184: Angel Number 184 appears when your spirit guides want you to increase your confidence. Something may have recently happened that left you questioning yourself and what you are really able to do. This is their reminder to you that you have a grounded way of approaching life and it is perfect for you, never forget that. All endings or failures do not mean anything against you.

185: Angel Number 185 brings a message from your spirit team of taking more of a childlike approach towards your daily work and responsibilities. You may be taking some things too seriously and are being summoned to enjoy yourself more while taking care of responsibilities.

186: Angel Number 186 appears in your life when your guides want you to take a deeper look into the role you have played in your current reality. By taking a realistic look at your life, you will be able to make well-informed decisions in the future that are grounded in lessons of the past. It's a reminder that we all have something to work on, we just need to make sure we are aware of what that is. It's time to think on what has been bothering you and take accountability for your role.

187: Angel Number 187 appears when your spirit guides are calling for you to take action on something you have been feeling is a good move to make. If you wait too long you may miss a good window of opportunity to strike gold.

188: Angel Number 188 is shown when your spirit guides feel you are ready to move into a new phase of your life. This phase will carry great responsibility, but they want you to be reminded that you were chosen for a reason. Allow yourself to show your leadership skills and go create magic! You are a natural leader and have great ideas that others would benefit from learning.

189: Angel Number 189 is shown to you when your spirit team feels as if you have outgrown a space that can no longer teach your or provide you with information to push you forward. You may be surrounded by people who know the same amount as you or less. Spirit wants you to seek more challenges at this time in your life that will enable you to keep growing.

190: Angel Number 190 appears in your life when your guides want you to know that you have been doing a great job at life. You are exiting a moment in your life and walking into unknown territory that will provide you with a breath of fresh air. The universe is working for your good!

191: Angel Number 191 shows up in your life when you are called to have more compassion for yourself at this time. You may have been hard on yourself about a situation, but your guides want you to know that it will all work out for you in the end. You are an alchemist and have the power to turn any situation into something different. All you have to do is put your energy and mind to it.

192: Angel Number 192 brings you encouragement regarding upcoming communication you are expecting from someone. Your guides want you to relax and know that the conversations will go smoothly and it will work out for your good. Express yourself carefully and concise to make sure you are heard properly.

193: Angel Number 193 appears when your spirit guides want you to get prepared for a move that is happening in your life. Whether you are moving jobs, homes, or even relationships; your guides want you to know that it will bring the stability you have been manifesting for quite some time. Everything is falling into alignment for you.

194: Angel Number 194 comes at a time when your guides want to give you hope for the future. The endings that have recently happened are setting you up for a major success moment. They want you to know that things had to happen this way because you were no longer making progress in this situation.

195: Angel Number 195 is a wakeup call from your spirit guides that it is time to move forward or you will get left behind in a particular area of your life. The changes that you are called to make will bring you greater wealth and emotional health. These changes have been a long time coming and know that you will be guided through the process as long as you are open to receiving the messages.

196: Angel Number 196 appears when you are ready to receive valuable information to help guide you through your next step on your spiritual journey. You had to have a difficult ending before you were found ready to receive this information. Whatever you do, do not allow it to go to waste or you will lose it. It will most likely be revealed to you in a dream or randomly in nature.

197: Angel Number 197 is shown when you are being called to change how you view information or people who think differently from you. You want to watch out for being judgmental, as they may be able to provide something that you need in the future.

198: Angel Number 198 appears when your guides want to remind you that you are the master of your fate and the captain of your soul. Nothing gets permission to affect you without first receiving your permission. Always remember that the only thing that will ever be able to bother you is what you allow yourself to be aroused by.

199: Angel Number 199 is a message of congratulations! Your guides are proud of you for taking the steps needed to end cycles in your life that were no longer suited for you. If you haven't you are being called to end cycles that have run its course. Whatever you do, make sure to forgive yourself for decisions you made when you weren't well-informed. It's a new day now.

Chapter 4: Angel Numbers 200-299

200: Angel Number 200 sends a message from your spirit guides to remind you that you are not alone. You have access to unlimited resources and help from your guides, all you have to do is keep an open mind.

201: Angel Number 201 appears when your spirit guides are calling for you to balance a situation you have with someone close to you. There may have been miscommunication that caused a disconnect that needs to be addressed and fixed.

202: Angel Number 202 appears when your spirit guides want you to realize the potential you and another person have together. At this time in your life, it is important for you to not put too many limitations or pressures on those who you are attached to. You can trust them even with space.

203: Angel Number 203 appears when your spirit guides want you to take a step back and brainstorm the best way to have a difficult conversation with someone in your life right now. It is important for you to address the situation if you want change to happen, you just want to make sure that it is received well.

204: Angel Number 204 comes to you when your guides want you to balance out your expectations in an unknown situation. The more balanced you are, the easier it will be to accept what happens and take it at face value.

205: Angel Number 205 appears when your guides are calling for you to connect with the unknown in order to bring about an important change in your personal life. You are called to be open to receive new information that will change your perspective and provide guidance on next steps on your journey.

206: *Angel Number 206* is here to let you know that your plans may not go as you want, but it will work out for your good in the end. You will find a hidden opportunity mixed in with disappointment. There is always a bright side at the end of the day; sometimes you have to look deeper to find it.

207: *Angel Number 207* brings a message from your guides reminding you of the power of your intuition. You have experienced various things in your life that have increased your personal instinct when it comes to judging new situations. Use that skill to just a situation you are currently involved in.

208: *Angel Number 208* is a message from your guides to not take everything so seriously right now. Plans won't always go accordingly and you have to be flexible when you are in positions of power or leadership.

209: *Angel Number 209* sends a message from your spirit guides to allow changes to happen in your life right now. They are happening in order to bring balance into your life. With the legal system, things will work out and lessons will be learned.

210: *Angel Number 210* appears when you are ready to take what you have learned from others and apply it to your life with no limitations. Allow yourself to be motivated by others and surround yourself with good energy.

211: *Angel Number 211* is here to remind you that we all need help at some point in our lives. It is ok to take help from others right now, especially if it relates to you becoming more stable in an area of your life.

212: *Angel Number 212* appears in your life when your spirit guides want you to know that you are currently being influenced heavily by other people and things right now. It may be smart to take inventory and only adopt behaviors that align with your soul and spirit.

213: Angel Number 213 brings a message from your spirit guides to be aware of how others are communicating with you right now. Watch the infliction of their voice and their body language. Someone may be saying one thing but their energy is giving something else. Your guides want you to go with the energy you are feeling.

214: Angel Number 214 appears in your life when you are being called to take notice of how much of your stability is dependent on someone or something else. You spirit guides want you to make sure you are not becoming too dependent on something or someone else when it comes to your personal growth and trusting your intuition.

215: Angel Number 215 comes to bring to your awareness how much you have changed recently after connecting with a certain person or group in your life. You are becoming more confident and your guides want you to celebrate more small wins in your life.

216: Angel Number 216 brings a message from your guides asking you to make well informed decisions that will work out well for you and those who you have a responsibility to. You are being called to be reflective on the best course of action you should take next.

217: Angel Number 217 is a message from your spirit guides to make sure you know who you are connecting with at this time of your life. You are in a vulnerable period of your life and you only want to have people attached to you who have your best interest at heart.

218: Angel Number 218 brings a message from your spirit guides to acknowledge information someone else shares with you. You are like a safe space to others and you will receive a secret from someone soon and your guides want you to make sure you don't share it with anyone else.

219: Angel Number 219 appears when you are preparing to walk away from someone or something that is no longer in alignment with who you are at this time in your life. When you are doing what is best for you know that it will be blessed.

220: Angel Number 220 appears when you are walking into a more calm time in your life. Although you may not be able to see into the future, your guides want you to know that you will be guided, protected, and at peace through the transition.

221: Angel Number 221 appears when your guides want you to be appreciated for life at this time. You have a lot to be grateful for at this moment, so take time to stop and say thank you to your guides for never leaving your side.

222: Angel Number 222 appears to let you know that you are in direct alignment with your soul purpose and your guides are pleased with the progress you have been making when it comes to keeping boundaries, staying calm in difficult situations, and remaining balanced.

223: Angel Number 223 appears when your guides are asking for you to partner with only those who have good intentions and good vibrations surrounding them. Move by what you can see tangibly and not just by how you feel.

224: Angel Number 224 appears in your life when your guides are reminding you of the importance of friendships in your life. Your friendships play a major role in your daily life and you want only those who are aligned with you in balance around you.

225: Angel Number 225 appears in your life when your guides are asking for you to make some changes in a current situation involving someone else. It has reached the end and it is time to either change the dynamics of your relationships together or call it quits.

226: Angel Number 226 appears when your guides are pushing for you to make more healthy choices and decisions that will provide you needed strength. What in your life has not been nurturing you? How can it be changed around to benefit?

227: Angel Number 227 sends a warning message from your spirit guides of balance. Whatever you are doing make sure you are providing equal time and energy to your responsibilities or one has the chance to overtake the other.

228: Angel Number 228: It is important for you to watch your communication at this time. Your words have the power to provide life or death so make sure you are choosing life unless you want to be the cause of another's fall. It's best to focus on you and where you are headed at this time.

229: Angel Number 229 Look to the stars at this time. You are being provided with an opportunity to show who you really are and what you have to offer the world Whatever you do, stick to your authentic self and allow yourself to be seen at this time.

230: Angel Number 230 It is important to take notice to your surroundings and what is going on in your situation right now before you move ahead too quickly. Anything can happen right now, so make sure you gather enough information to make a well-informed decision.

231: Angel Number 231 Balance of your mind, emotions, and spirit is important at this time. It is important to know how the communication from others affects you and your personal confidence at this time. Know that you are the only person whose opinion matters at this time. Take their advice and make your own final decision.

232: Angel Number 232 Follow your intuition at this time. You will not go wrong and your spirit guides want you to know that you are in alignment with your purpose. You can't go wrong right now so keep walking into your abundance.

233: Angel Number 233 You have been preparing for a new beginning for quite some time and it is now being manifested before your eyes. Whatever you do, seize the opportunity and allow yourself to bask in what is to come.

234: Angel Number 234 Your current connections with others are very instrumental in your success at this time. This is not the time to run and hide from the world, yet put yourself out there and allow your guides to introduce you to others who are in alignment with your purpose. Your blessings come through stable relationships with others at this time.

235: Angel Number 235 The end of a tough cycle is approaching and your spirit guides want you to know that this is not the time to quit and give up. After this karmic cycle passes you will feel like yourself again. Keep going.

236: Angel Number 236 Your spirit guides want you to be careful with what information you share with others and what you decide to keep to yourself. This is a reminder to only share what needs to be shared and to not offer information that someone has not been made privy to be aware of.

237: Angel Number 237 This is a reminder from your guides to keep going. You have many people amazed at how far you have come in life. Especially those who weren't expecting you to. Keep making them believers without trying. Keep being you.

238: Angel Number 238 There is so much opportunity in front of you and your guides want you to keep an open mind at this time. You may be in a time of planning for future actions. Stay hopeful and know you will find the perfect fit for you at this time.

239: Angel Number 239 Your attitude at this time determines the altitude in which you continue to climb. It is important for you to see the bright side of any endings that are currently happening in order to keep manifesting good energy in your space.

240: Angel Number 240 A new stable connection is enroute of you at this time. You are being rewarded for staying focused on your goals by not being distracted by the outside world. A new opportunity is being made available to you as you are fertile for growth at this time.

241: Angel Number 241 If it is not aligned with what you are working on right now it is important to say no. Your guides want you to know that time and energy is very valuable right now and you need to preserve yours for what deserves it at this time.

242: Angel Number 242 Your stability is being affected by someone else at this time whether you realize it or not. It is important that you make sure to keep peace in your relationships at this time or you may be forced to take over a responsibility you weren't prepared for.

243: Angel Number 243 Your spirit guides want you to consider traveling to a new place in order to gain a deeper understanding of life around you. It is time to face your fears and do something out of the ordinary in order to create compassion for others you didn't previously understand.

244: Angel Number 244 Someone is currently being placed under judgment at this time. If it is you judging someone else, make sure the judgments are warranted. If it is you, the other person is coming to the realization that they were too harsh on you with their judgments.

245: Angel Number 245 appears when your guides want you to look at a situation from another perspective. You may have recently been disappointed by someone or something and they want you to know that sometimes things happen and someone is at the brunt end. It had nothing to do with you personally, it just so happened that you were collateral damage.

246: Angel Number 246 appears when your guides want you to pay more attention to your mental health at this time. It is important that you keep a positive mindset towards your difficulties at this time and not allow anxiety or depression to take over.

247: Angel Number 247 appears when your guides feel you are ready to take a walk into unknown territory. You have gained much knowledge over time and it is time to put what you have learned into practice.

248: Angel Number 248 appears when your guides want you to take a break and enjoy yourself. You have been working really hard lately alone and it is a good time to take a break, go for some dancing, or just spend some time with close friends having fun with no work.

249: *Angel Number 249* brings a message from your spirit guides to allow endings to happen. There is no need to try and stop something from happening when it was always inevitable. Just let it flow.

250: *Angel Number 250* appears when your guides want you to walk with more confidence at this time in your life. You have a lot to offer and what makes you unique is that there is only one of you. Allow yourself to embrace your uniqueness and have fun doing so.

251: *Angel Number 251* appears when your guides want you to know that you have divine protection around you and it is ok to be a free spirit without self-sabotage at this time. Do not limit yourself right now... Your guides want you to feel free!

252: *Angel Number 252* appears when your guides want you to balance out your child-like energy and adulthood. With proper balance you are then allowed to be your total complete self without feeling like you are neglecting any part of yourself.

253: *Angel Number 253* appears when your guides are calling for you to pay attention to your responsibilities more. Make sure you are in alignment with the goals you have set for yourself. If you are not working towards them, then you are not aligned right now.

254: *Angel Number 254* appears when your guides want you to allow someone else to show up and take care of you for a moment. You have been doing alot and it is ok to let someone else take over and share the workload. It's ok to be taken care of at times.

255: *Angel Number 255* appears when your guides are calling for you to learn from someone else how to do something you are interested in. You are currently a novice and they want to remind you that practice and learning from trained individuals is what will make your learning perfect at this time.

***256:** Angel Number 256* appears when your guides want you to know that you can trust a new person that is in your energy right now. If you have been questioning if you should continue connecting with someone, this is clarification that they are not here to cause you harm unless they have shown you otherwise.

***257:** Angel Number 257* shows up when your guides want to remind you that the things you experienced in your childhood all aided in who you have become today as an older individual. They also want you to know that you can choose to continue living through that experience or choose to create a new experience.

***258:** Angel Number 258* shows up when your guides want you to take more charge in your day to day life. There is an area where you are leaving things up to chance and your guides want for you to actually control the direction and flow of it.

***259:** Angel Number 259* shows up when your guides want you to reconsider some of your current alliances. Whoever you are attached to right now have to be aligned with your purpose or you run the risk of being affected by the discord.

***260:** Angel Number 260* appears when your guides are calling for you to protect your vision as you are working on it. If you share your ideas too soon, you run the risk of them being tainted by someone with negative energy.

***261:** Angel Number 261* appears when you are being called to create more boundaries in your relationships. You have been giving too freely of yourself which has been draining your energy left over for yourself. Time to balance it out.

***262:** Angel Number 262* appears when you are going through a period of judgment from the universe. At this time, your energy is being measured to see how pure your intentions are at this time. If you are engaged with something that is harmful to others, it is important to take an honest look at it and your involvement.

263: Angel Number 263 appears when your guides want you to pay more attention to the communication that is being had between you and the youth around you. Make sure you are feeding life into them and encouraging them as they learn themselves in relationships to the world. You are more influential than you may realize.

264: Angel Number 264 appears when you are being called to get focused on what you need to do right now. Distractions can come easy and it's imperative that you know how to stay grounded so they don't sweep you off your purpose.

265: Angel Number 265 appears when your guides are calling for you to be a little warmer with someone in your life right now. You want to watch out for defensiveness with people as a result of your past trauma. If they haven't shown you they aren't trustworthy, do not allow your trauma to interfere.

266: Angel Number 266 appears when it is time for you to get your financial books in order. You may have some big purchases coming up and your guides want you to make sure you are organized and prepared for whatever may happen right now unexpectedly.

267: Angel Number 267 appears when your spirit guides want you to do research on your current eating habits and diet. If you have been gaining weight or having health issues, they want you to start with analyzing what you have been eating, start cutting back on the culprit, and adopt healthier alternatives.

268: Angel Number 268 appears when your spirit guides want you to use your best judgment when it comes to jumping into a new business or financial endeavor. You want to make sure this investment has a strong potential of providing financial stability and gains in the future.

***269:* Angel Number 269** appears when you are being called to balance out your responsibilities and to cut out anything that is not in alignment with your current purpose or personal needs. It is simply a distraction at this time.

***270:* Angel Number 270** brings a message of concern from your spirit guides. You may have had an overactive imagination or crown chakra at this time and they want you to make sure you have your heart and throat chakra in alignment as well. By balancing your heart and how you voice your needs, a new perspective will arise.

***271:* Angel Number 271** brings a message of self-sustainability at this time. It is important that you do not depend too much on someone else to provide you with guidance and knowledge. If you need to know which to choose, research it on your own first.

***272:* Angel Number 272** brings a message from your spirit guides letting you know that they are watching over you and are sending new information your way that will help you with a current problem you are facing. Stay hopeful and know that you will always be divinely protected.

***273:* Angel Number 273** appears when your guides want you to know that you do not have to handle everything alone. By calling on your guides and asking for help, they are able to send you exactly what you need to take a weight off your shoulders.

***274:* Angel Number 274** appears when your guides want you to take notice of all that is available to you right now. You have the ability to dream and create the reality you want right now, just make sure you are doing the proper work and research to aid in the process.

***275:* Angel Number 275** appears when your guides are asking you to be more understanding of people who think or feel differently from you. You have different upbringings and by understanding how they operate and how to work with them, it will help you in future endeavors when you encounter other people like them.

276: Angel Number 276 appears when your guides want you to learn more emotional intelligence. It is important to not allow yourself to become too aroused by the actions or emotions of others.

277: Angel Number 277 appears when your guides are urging you to connect more with nature and what she has to offer you right now. The more knowledgeable you become about mother earth, the more connected you will be with the web of life and humanity.

278: Angel Number 278 appears when your spirit guides are calling for you to take a break, breathe, and allow yourself to adjust to the current changes in your life. After your break, you will feel a second wind under your wings.

279: Angel Number 279 brings a message from your spirit guides to not be afraid to end something in order to build something else that is stronger and better. It could be a relationship or a home. Something better comes after an ending of something that no longer suits you. Thank it for its service in your life and move forward.

280: Angel Number 280 appears when your spirit guide wants you to know that you have a team of people behind you rooting for you, whether you see them or not. You have people who want to see you succeed so only focus on that energy right now.

281: Angel Number 281 appears when your guides are calling for you to connect yourself with resources that aid in what you are currently working on or looking for more information on. When you seek, you find. It's time to be a detective.

282: Angel Number 282 appears when your spirit guides are calling for you to find a mentor to help you with this new phase of your life that you are walking into. They will help you understand new ways to manage your current responsibilities and new roles that are enroute of you right now.

276: ***Angel Number 276*** appears when your guides want you to learn more emotional intelligence. It is important to not allow yourself to become too aroused by the actions or emotions of others.

277: ***Angel Number 277*** appears when your guides are urging you to connect more with nature and what she has to offer you right now. The more knowledgeable you become about mother earth, the more connected you will be with the web of life and humanity.

278: ***Angel Number 278*** appears when your spirit guides are calling for you to take a break, breathe, and allow yourself to adjust to the current changes in your life. After your break, you will feel a second wind under your wings.

279: ***Angel Number 279*** brings a message from your spirit guides to not be afraid to end something in order to build something else that is stronger and better. It could be a relationship or a home. Something better comes after an ending of something that no longer suits you. Thank it for its service in your life and move forward.

280: ***Angel Number 280*** appears when your spirit guide wants you to know that you have a team of people behind you rooting for you, whether you see them or not. You have people who want to see you succeed so only focus on that energy right now.

281: ***Angel Number 281*** appears when your guides are calling for you to connect yourself with resources that aid in what you are currently working on or looking for more information on. When you seek, you find. It's time to be a detective.

282: ***Angel Number 282*** appears when your spirit guides are calling for you to find a mentor to help you with this new phase of your life that you are walking into. They will help you understand new ways to manage your current responsibilities and new roles that are enroute of you right now.

283: Angel Number 283 shows up when you need to be reminded of the divine power you have inside of you. You are a power magician and it is important that you protect that part of yourself at all times, especially if you are consistently around others who have a hard time manifesting.

284: Angel Number 284 appears when your guides want you to remember that you were once a child who had to learn right from wrong. Make sure you are extending the same grace you once needed for others around you who are learning lessons you have already mastered.

285: Angel Number 285 appears when your guides want you to speak up more in a situation. You may have been silent due to feeling like you are not worthy of the knowledge you possess, but this is a reminder that you deserve to be in whatever position or space you are in. Do not allow others to intimidate you.

286: Angel Number 286 is here to warn you that someone sees you as competition at this time in your life. It is important to know that no one starts conflict with someone whom they aren't threatened by. Take it as a complement and ignore their advances. It is above you.

287: Angel Number 287 appears when your guides want you to go for something you feel is out of reach. It is hard to grow when you are playing it safe, allow yourself to dream big and have the courage to put yourself out there for new opportunities. You never know what will happen after a while.

288: Angel Number 288 is here to remind you that your spirit guides want you to live and walk in your complete truth. No matter what, do not allow someone else to define who you are and your experiences. Only you can do that. You have a spirit team that is fighting for your at this moment.

289: Angel Number 289 appears when you are being called to have compassion for someone in a leadership role at this time. They may have made a bad decision that affected many others and your guides want you to be the one to have compassion for them at this time. You just may need someone on your team in the future as well.

283: Angel Number 283 shows up when you need to be reminded of the divine power you have inside of you. You are a power magician and it is important that you protect that part of yourself at all times, especially if you are consistently around others who have a hard time manifesting.

284: Angel Number 284 appears when your guides want you to remember that you were once a child who had to learn right from wrong. Make sure you are extending the same grace you once needed for others around you who are learning lessons you have already mastered.

285: Angel Number 285 appears when your guides want you to speak up more in a situation. You may have been silent due to feeling like you are not worthy of the knowledge you possess, but this is a reminder that you deserve to be in whatever position or space you are in. Do not allow others to intimidate you.

286: Angel Number 286 is here to warn you that someone sees you as competition at this time in your life. It is important to know that no one starts conflict with someone whom they aren't threatened by. Take it as a complement and ignore their advances. It is above you.

287: Angel Number 287 appears when your guides want you to go for something you feel is out of reach. It is hard to grow when you are playing it safe, allow yourself to dream big and have the courage to put yourself out there for new opportunities. You never know what will happen after a while.

288: Angel Number 288 is here to remind you that your spirit guides want you to live and walk in your complete truth. No matter what, do not allow someone else to define who you are and your experiences. Only you can do that. You have a spirit team that is fighting for your at this moment.

289: Angel Number 289 appears when you are being called to have compassion for someone in a leadership role at this time. They may have made a bad decision that affected many others and your guides want you to be the one to have compassion for them at this time. You just may need someone on your team in the future as well.

290: Angel Number 290 appears when your spirit guides want you to allow others to be themselves fully without judgment. You may be surrounded by people who differ from you. It doesn't mean something is wrong with them, it just means they are different and its important to understand how to work with people who are different from you without trying to change them.

291: Angel Number 291 brings a message from your guides to welcome endings with open arms. There is an ending in your life that is making way for a new creative endeavor that you have been praying and preparing for. Allow it to happen.

292: Angel Number 292 appears when your guides are ready for you to evolve into a newer version of yourself. Where have you been trying to stop a change from happening? This is a reminder that some endings need to happen in order to be connected with something more aligned with you and your purpose.

293: Angel Number 293 appears when your guides are calling for you to take more control of your life at this time. It is important to gauge what is going on, so you can keep everything in alignment with your purpose and what you are currently manifesting. Whatever is interfering needs to go.

294: Angel Number 294 appears when you are being called to accept all sides of yourself. You have dark and light inside of you and when they are balanced is when you find yourself elevating more. You'll find some many respect you more when you embrace your dark energy as well (such as boundaries which come from dark energy).

295: Angel Number 295 appears when your spirit guides want you to begin taking action. You may have been taking an extended break and they want you to know that the time has come for you to jump back into the world full force!

296: Angel Number 296 appears when your spirit team want to remind you that when doors close, it just means it was no longer suitable for you. The doors you are meant to walk through will open with no difficulty or problem.

***297:** Angel Number 297* shows up when you are being called to forgive others and yourself for things that were done while in an energy of deficiency. Forgiveness of self is what's most important. Use the experience to guide your next actions and move on.

***298:** Angel Number 298* appears when your spirit guides want you to create more boundaries when it comes to having access to you. When the wrong people have access to you, they can potentially affect your magic and manifestations. Cut the leeches off.

***299:** Angel Number 299* appears when your guides are calling for you to go through a total life makeover. It's time to take a look at your mental, emotional, physical, and spiritual self and dump what is no longer in alignment with the new you. Similar to spring cleaning... get rid of the old to make room for the new.

Chapter 5: Angel Numbers 300-399

300: Angel Number 300 shows up when you are entering a strong manifestation period of your life. It is important that you direct your attention, thoughts, and words in the direction of what you are manifesting because this energy has not been tamed yet and can be tricked if you allow negative energy to get in the way.

301: Angel Number 301 appears when your spirit guides want you to speak what you want into existence. Anything you want is available to you as long as you believe and are in alignment with whatever you are manifesting.

302: Angel Number 302 appears when your spirit guides want you to see the unlimited options you have around you at this time. Choose wisely because the option you choose will have an impact on your personal success.

303: Angel Number 303 appears when your spirit guides are telling you to not limit yourself and your potential. This is a strong manifesting time for you and it is important for you to be intentional with your intentions, thoughts, and how you spend your time. It's very valuable!

304: Angel Number 304 appears when your spirit guides are asking for you to shift your perception of what stability looks and feels like. You may be operating off outdated beliefs and your guides want you to make sure you are not limiting yourself with old beliefs or information.

305: Angel Number 305 appears when your spirit guides are asking you to make a change in your work life that will benefit you in the long run. If you are looking for a raise or more money, it's time to start networking and putting yourself out there to allow opportunities the chance to show themselves.

306: Angel Number 306 appears when your spirit guides want you to pay attention to how you get your point across with others. Communication is key right now and you don't want to push someone away who could be an ally to you in the long-run.

307: Angel Number 307 appears when your spirit guides want you to see your true worth. You may be downplaying yourself and are being called to shift perception of who you are in the context of your inner circles and community. You are more valuable than you may notice.

308: Angel Number 308 appears when your spirit guides are letting you know that an increase of wealth is headed your way! Your hard work is paying off and the universe is working to bless you for what you have done in the past. Good karma is enroute to you!

309: Angel Number 309 appears when your spirit guides are letting you know that the endings that are currently happening in your life were all divinely guided in order to make room for what you really want. Your guides had to remove it all for a reason.

310: Angel Number 310 appears when you are being called to control your tongue. Just because you think it doesn't mean it is meant for you to share it out with others. Silence is golden right now.

311: Angel Number 311 appears when your spirit guides want for you to clear the air regarding a disappointment you've recently experienced with someone. If you feel comfortable, share it with them. If not, keep it to yourself and change how you deal with them.

312: Angel Number 312 appears when you are in need of some fresh air at this time. Your spirit guides want you to get outside and breathe in some clear air and it will help you clear your mind of any brain fogs you have been experiencing.

313: Angel Number 313 shows up in your life when your guides want you to guide your thoughts in the direction of creative thinking. Instead of thinking about the past, change your thoughts to what you can create in the future that will be more beneficial to you.

314: Angel Number 314 appears when your spirit guides are asking for you to stand in your power and up for what you know is right for you at this time. It is ok to say no to whatever you do not want to do.

315: Angel Number 315 appears when your spirit guides want you to take a step back and analyze a situation that has been stagnant. They are asking for you to look at why it has been stagnant in order to identify what needs to be changed in order to allow it to flow again.

316: Angel Number 316 appears when your spirit guides are asking you to take a more creative approach to getting your point across at this time. You are being called to think outside of the box in order to get others to go along with your plan and support it.

317: Angel Number 317 appears in your life when your guides are asking for you to take a step back and analyze what is going on in your life right now. Are you happy with the direction you are walking in? If not, it's time to start researching a new way to approach what is not in alignment with your vibe.

318: Angel Number 318 appears in your life when your guides are calling for you to be patient as you work towards something. It may seem like things are moving along for others and not you. Use this time to celebrate them and know that your turn is on its way. Keep working on your craft.

319: Angel Number 319 appears in your life when your spirit guides are calling for you to make sure you are not allowing the opinions and thoughts of others to influence your personal decisions.

320: Angel Number 320 appears in your life when your spirit guides want you to remember that all things are working out for your good. The universe is always helping you, just make sure you are creating the boundaries required for you to receive it.

321: Angel Number 321 appears in your life when your spirit guides want you to know that the wheel of fortune is turning in your favor at this time in your life. Get prepared for a big surprise that will be showing itself really soon in your life!

322: Angel Number 322 appears when your spirit guides are calling for you to spend more time with your ancestral team. There is some wisdom and information you can gain by calling on them and their support.

323 Angel Number 323 shows up when your spirit guides are putting you in alignment with a divine partnership. This partnership will be used to propel you forward in your career, creative pursuits, and communication skills. It will be a benevolent time.

324: Angel Number 324 shows up when your spirit guides want you to know that you have a lot of power to change your current situation that isn't bringing you joy. You have all of the ingredients and information needed, all you need to do is act on it.

325: Angel Number 325 appears when your spirit guides want you to know that someone around you needs to speak up and share with you how they are really feeling about your relationship. Get prepared for the conversation and have an open mind.

326: Angel Number 326 appears when your spirit guides want you to trust the judgment you have made about a situation or person in your life. You have experienced a lot and can trust that you will make a wise decision that is best for you.

327: Angel Number 327 appears when your spirit guides want you to increase your boundaries and access to you. You may have been allowing others too much access to you and their energy is draining you at this time. Pull back and become more selective at this time.

328: Angel Number 328 appears when your spirit guides want you to put your foot down in a situation. You said what you said and this is your sign to let you know that you are not seeing things incorrectly at this time.

329: Angel Number 329 appears when your spirit guides want you to change something up from your daily routine. If you want different results, you can't keep doing the same thing.

330: Angel Number 330 comes into your life when your spirit guides are preparing to send someone in your life who has similar thoughts, feelings, and perceptions about the world. You can expect to have this person in your life for quite some time whether as friends or lovers. It will happen unexpectedly.

331: Angel Number 331 appears when your spirit guides want you to take notice of how others are communicating with you. If your spirit doesn't like it, there is a reason for that and you should take heed.

332: Angel Number 332 appears when your spirit guides want you to know that people are listening to you and taking what you say seriously, so make sure you are being authentic and understand just how powerful your words are!

333: Angel Number 333 appears when your spirit guides feel you are ready to receive divine knowledge about something esoteric. It is important for you to pay attention to what you are listening to or talking about when you see 333, because the clues are found there. You are a powerful manifester so use the information you gain to push forward.

334: Angel Number 334 shows itself when your guides are ready for you to embrace the newness of new information you have recently received. After applying it, you will notice a change in your mood, energy, and the energy of others in your space.

335: Angel Number 335 appears when your spirit guides want for you to take what you have learned from your work environment and incorporate it into something that allows you to be more creative.

336: Angel Number 336 appears in your life when your spirit guides are trying to get your attention to focus on your health. It's time to connect with others who are on a similar journey as you when it comes to your health goals.

337: Angel Number 337 appears in your life when your spirit guides are calling for you to document knowledge you have obtained over the years. This could be a book documenting a personal experience or informational guide that can help others grow in an area of their life.

338: Angel Number 338 shows up in your life when your spirit guides are requesting your presence. They would like for you to spend more time in solitude to make sure the energy you are currently receiving or feeling is a result of your own vibrations or someone attached to you.

339: Angel Number 339 brings a message of awareness. Your spirit guides want you to look at how you communicate your needs to others in your circle. Are you being honest about what it is you need? You are your greatest spokesperson, so make sure you are speaking up when needed.

340: Angel Number 340 reveals itself to you when your spirit guides want to remind you that mental health is very important. When you do not focus on maintaining your emotional and mental self, you run the risk of going rogue without warning. Grounding is key in your life right now.

341: Angel Number 341 appears when your spirit guides want for you to use new knowledge you have acquired and apply it to your life currently. This new knowledge will set you up to become more of the main character in your life.

342: Angel Number 342 appears when your spirit guides want you to stop caring so much about what other people think or feel about you. Their opinion has nothing to do with your life, so make sure you are not internalizing things that do not relate to you. Use your intuition more.

343: Angel Number 343 appears in your life when your spirit guides are calling for you to look into connecting with brighter colors at this time. By adding a little color to your day, you will notice a mood shift.

344: Angel Number 344 appears in your life when your spirit guides are ready for you to take action towards something you have been planning for quite some time. They want you to know that you will be protected as you step out on faith. Whatever you do, stay confident and keep your boundaries for ultimate protection and success.

345: Angel Number 345 appears in your life when your guides want to relay a message of hope to you. You have made some changes recently in your life and they want you to know that everything happens in diving timing. You may not see the end of the rope right now, but as you keep walking forward it all becomes more visible over time.

346: Angel Number 346 shows up in your life when your guides want you to be prepared for someone returning from your past. This is a connection that ended due to immaturity and lack of stability. Your spirit guides are providing you both another opportunity to build a connection on solid ground. Take it slow.

347: Angel Number 347 appears in your life when your spirit guides want you to remember why you made certain decisions in the past. Do not question why or beat yourself up. You used what you had to make the best decision for what you needed at that time.

348: Angel Number 348 shows up in your life when your spirit guides want for you to take control over an issue in your personal life. You may be leaving something up for chance too much, disabling your ability to guide the direction you need to be moving in.

349: Angel Number 349 shows up to remind you that there is no such thing as luck, luck is simply just the manifestation of being in a space you were supposed to be at, at the right time. You are lucky when you do things you are intuitively drawn towards and end things your spirit tells you no longer has benefit to you.

350: Angel Number 350 appears when you are called to use your imagination to create something new. It doesn't need to have an end goal, just create and be amazed by the final project. This can be through art, writing, dancing, whatever! You are the blueprint and your guides want for you to create a masterpiece.

351: Angel Number 351 appears when your guides want to motivate and remind you that you are divinely protected in whatever endeavor you choose to walk into. Even if you change your mind 1000 times, they are still there to support you as long as you are doing something that makes your soul feel free.

352: Angel Number 352 appears when your guides are calling for you to take notice of others around you who have your back. You may have been having a pessimistic mindset towards something or someone recently and your guides want you to remember that there are people in our corner rooting for you to win. Focus on them and not the naysayers.

353: Angel Number 353 appears in your life when your spirit guides want you to change how you have been viewing situations that appear to be negative at first glance. By transmuting the difficult moments and losses into a positive, you become an alchemist and are able to benefit from it.

354: Angel Number 354 appears when your spirit guides are calling for you to change your perception of your home life situation. How can you be more positive about your current life and situation? When you find beauty in difficult situations you are telling your guides that you are open to receiving more.

355: Angel Number 355 shows up when your guides are calling for you to try different things to find what you like at this period of your life. Do not limit yourself or your creativity. You will never know if you like it or not if you never try.

***356:** Angel Number 356* shows up when your spirit guides are calling for you to create a new organized schedule for yourself and your household. Recently there have been some changes and your guides want you to adjust so you are able to stay on top of everything properly.

***357:** Angel Number 357* appears in your life when your spirit guides want for you to choose happiness no matter what is going on in your life right now. When you choose to be happy few things will be able to affect your mood, how you move, and your thoughts.

***358:** Angel Number 358* appears when your spirit guides want for you to address hidden feelings or thoughts that you haven't allowed yourself to address or assess. They want you to know that it is important for you to have a healthy outlet to process your thoughts and feelings in order to make sense of it all and not repeat it.

***359:** Angel Number 359* shows up in your life when your spirit guides want for you to make a difficult decision that will cause an ending to something you have become comfortable with. A period of stagnation is coming to an end by shaking up the foundation and allowing yourself to enter into a territory where you are able to grow even more.

***360:** Angel Number 360* appears in your life when your spirit guides are calling for you to take a look around you to take inventory of your life and the surrounding energy. By looking around you, it allows you the opportunity to make informed decisions in the next phase of your life.

***361:** Angel Number 361* shows up when your spirit guides want you to get ready for your life to turn around! Just when you thought life was getting boring, stagnant, or not fun enough, you are going to find yourself getting busier and more active.

***362:** Angel Number 362* is a message from your spirit guides to remind you that anything can happen at any time so it is important that you stay ready for whatever. The more prepared you are on the front end, the more joyous you will be as you make the transition.

363: Angel Number 363 is a message from your spirit guides letting you know that your hard work has not been in vain. You possess a creative energy inside of you that others would love to have, so make sure you are continuously nurturing your gifts that make you unique.

364: Angel Number 364 is here to remind you that you are your biggest investment. You are being called to take some time to nurture and pamper yourself. It's not fair to expect others to do things that you wouldn't do for yourself. Time to do things that you want from others.

365: Angel Number 365 appears in your life when your spirit guides want you to take a moment to see how far you have come over the last year. You may have not been giving enough credit to yourself and your growth. You have a lot to be proud of and grateful for!

366: Angel Number 366 appears in your life when your spirit guides want for you to start something new that you can do every day for the next year. This new process will help you get more organized and teach the discipline needed to manage something bigger that is on its way to you.

367: Angel Number 367 shows up in your life when your guides want for you to take note of the generational curses that you have been breaking in your family and the generational blessings you are creating.

368: Angel Number 368 appears in your life when your spirit guides are calling for you to create a new schedule that will enable you to have more control over your time and energy. This is not a good time to just go with the flow in your life; yet organize it to how it works best for you and your productivity.

369: Angel Number 369 shows up in your life when your guides want you to realize how abundantly creative and fertile you are. You have the ability to create anything and turn it into gold when you put all of our energy and dedication into it. You bring life to everything you touch.

370: Angel Number 370 appears in your life when your spirit guides are ready to give you new esoteric knowledge that carry power that can be used for good or bad. This information will be found in your dreams or a book that will be recommended to you in the next 7 days.

371: Angel Number 371 shows up when your spirit guides want you to allow something that is no longer working for you to die out. When you stop giving attention to it, it eventually dies out and you will eventually no longer think about it.

372: Angel Number 372 shows itself to you when your spirit guides want you to start brainstorming out an idea that has been given to you. There is no need to worry, just take your time and allow it all to unfold as you devote your time and energy to it.

373: Angel Number 373 shows up in your life when your spirit guides want you to remember how valuable you are to those around you. There are many people who depend on your good benevolent energy. Do not forget to take time to rest and recharge.

374: Angel Number 374 appears in your life when you need to be reminded of just how valuable you are to the world around you. Many people want to see you succeed and are rooting for you!

375: Angel Number 375 shows up when you are called to embrace new information you have received. This new information contradicts what you have known up until this point of your life. Your guides want you to embrace it and allow yourself to continue expanding.

376: Angel Number 376 appears when your spirit guides want you to be open for a new opportunity that is about to present itself in your life. You are called to allow your star power to shine as you walk into it.

377: Angel Number 377 appears in your life when your spirit guides want you to consult a wise individual to help you with an issue you are having related to your emotional health. This can be related to your family, love partnership, or personal spiritual growth.

378: *Angel Number 378* shows up when you are being called to share your expertise with others who can benefit from your knowledge and guidance.

379: *Angel Number 379* reveals itself when you are being called to become more knowledgeable about a situation that could be sensitive to some. As you get more knowledge you will approach this situation from a different perspective.

380: *Angel Number 380* shows up in your life when your spirit guides want you to embrace your big boss energy. You have characteristic traits in you that no one else around you have. Use them!

381: *Angel Number 381* appears in your life when your spirit guides are calling for you to be a little selfish to get what you need. It's important to know when you must put yourself first in order to reach your personal goals.

382: *Angel Number 382* shows up in your life when you are being called to allow someone into your space to work on a project together. You are currently working on something that would be stronger if you had help.

383: *Angel Number 383* appears in your life when your spirit guides are encouraging you to get out and enjoy yourself in the midst of good company. This is not the time to separate yourself from people, yet find people who align with your purpose. You are divinely protected from people who don't mean well for you.

384: *Angel Number 384* shows up in your life when your spirit guides are asking you to take your time with something you are creating if you want it to have lasting power. Good things take time.

385: *Angel Number 385* shows up when you are being called to take a creative approach towards your manifestations. By changing one thing you will notice a swift change in your immediate energy.

386: Angel Number 386 appears when your spirit guides want you to slow down and take note of all the good things around you. You may be focusing on lower energy and you are being called to raise your vibration by seeing the good things around you.

387: Angel Number 387 appears when your spirit guides want to let you know that justice is on its way to you. Things are working out in your favor and all that was lost will be given back to you 10-fold.

388: Angel Number 388 shows up in your life when your spirit guides are creating a space for you to show up and flourish. Use this time to connect with your spirit team and let them know exactly what you need from them to bring success.

389: Angel Number 389 appears in your life when your spirit guides are calling for you to upgrade your appearance in some way. This change will increase your confidence and visibility to others to attract the attention you need to push something further.

390: Angel Number 390 shows up when your spirit guides are calling for you to tap into your intuition more. You may have been trying to understand things from a logical perspective, when you need to look at it from more of an intuitive spiritual perspective.

391: Angel Number 391 shows itself in your life when you are being called to trust yourself more. When you make a decision, know that you did what you felt was best for you. Have no regrets.

392: Angel Number 392 appears in your life when you are preparing to embark on a new journey. Your spirit guides are reminding you to remain balanced and calm in unknown territory. You got this!

393: Angel Number 393 shows up when your spirit guides want you to take a serious look into what may be causing any creative blockages you are having at this time. It may be a good idea to write out your thoughts as a way to better identify what is going on in your energy.

394: Angel Number 394 appears when your spirit guides want you to forgive someone for something they did against you. By starting the process of forgiveness, you are opening up more opportunities for you because the negative energy of unforgiveness is no longer attached to you.

395: Angel Number 395 appears when your spirit guides want you to do something you don't always do. This sporadic change of activity will increase your energy, which will then translate into the enrichment of your life and abundance.

396: Angel Number 396 appears when your spirit guides want you to be attentive to your surroundings. If someone or something doesn't feel right, they want you to pay more attention to those feelings to see where they are coming from.

397: Angel Number 397 shows up in your life when your spirit guides are calling for you to talk to them more about life and what has been going on. The exchange of energy between you all will prove to be beneficial because it would not only make you feel connected, you will also feel like you have learned something new by brainstorming out your thoughts and feelings.

398: Angel Number 398 appears when your spirit guides want for you to sit back and learn from watching how someone else does something. By watching them work you will find new motivation of how to handle a situation you were previously stumped over.

399: Angel Number 399 appears in your life when you are called to take a break to allow your brain to rest and creative juices to build up. After this break, you will find yourself with a boost of creative energy that flows.

Chapter 6: Angel Numbers 400-499

400: Angel Number 400 shows up in your life when your spirit guides want you to get ready for your foundation to get shaken up! You asked for this, so buckle up and prepare for the ride it will be an adventurous one!

401: Angel Number 401 appears in your life when your spirit guides are calling for you to embrace the energy you bring to spaces when you enter a room. Your energy is so defined that you can turn a dark space light and a light space dark if you want to. Choose wisely.

402: Angel Number 402 shows up in your life when you are being called to find a way to merge different sides of yourself into one. This is not a time to hide parts of yourself. If you want others to love all of you, they have to know what all of you entail.

403: Angel Number 403 shows up when your guides want you to see how you can liven up your living space more. You may be called to look into feng shui or even add some color to the walls in your home in order to awaken your creative energy.

404: Angel Number 404 appears in your life when your guides want you to prioritize the protection of your home and workspace at this time. Boundaries are really important and you want to make sure you are comfortable in your safe space.

405: Angel Number 405 appears in your life when you are looking into moving to a new home or moving rooms around in one of your spaces. Whatever it is, your spirit guides want you to know that the time is now to start the process.

406: Angel Number 406 appears in your life when you need to take a look at the boundaries you have put into place with your schedule and responsibilities. You want to make sure that there aren't any gaps or potential for distractions.

407: Angel Number 407 is revealed to you when you are ready to start learning something new, like skill or increase of knowledge. Whatever you do, start slow and do not try to do too much too soon. Enjoy the process.

408: Angel Number 408 is revealed to you when your spirit guides want you to remember that you have overcome so much in your life. Whenever you are faced with adversity, remember how much you have gotten through in the past. Nothing is too hard for you.

409: Angel Number 409 shows up when it is time to purge items from your home, workspace, or personal life in general that no longer work for your good. If you do not like the energy of it; it has to go!

410: Angel Number 410 brings you a message of hope. Although you can't see the future, your guides want you to remember that you have the power to create the future that you want. All you have to do is start taking the actions that lead you towards what you want.

411: Angel Number 411 shows up when your spirit guides want you to take notice of information you will be receiving soon. Some of the information will sound like gossip, but there are details in it that will help you with something you are preparing to do.

412: Angel Number 412 appears when your spirit guides want you to keep some information for yourself. You do not need to reveal all of your secrets to others, it's good to keep an air of mystery to you.

413: Angel Number 413 sends a message from your spirit guides to take some time away from your home if you have been feeling stagnant with your work or creative juices. You can take a vacation or just visit a local art gallery for inspiration.

414: Angel Number 414 appears when your spirit guides want you to find your stability in a world that wants you to be unstable. What works for you is for you and it's important to stand on your word and not wander.

415: Angel Number 415 appears when your spirit guides are calling for you to protect your childlike faith and innocence from others who are unbelievers. You may be surrounded by people who want you to act a certain way. Always choose yourself first.

416: Angel Number 416 brings a message from your spirit guides to stay focused on the plan you have set forth for yourself at this time. Even if it seems like it's not working, it will all makes sense in the end.

417: Angel Number 417 brings a message from your spirit guides to get more connected with your living space. How do you feel when you are home? It may be time to research how to bring more positive energy in your home.

418: Angel Number 418 appears when your spirit guides want you to stand on the authority that has been given to you. You are being called to stand firm and be immovable as others around you may be seeking to diminish your reputation or leadership.

419: Angel Number 419 appears when your spirit guides want you to get prepared for a shift in your stability. You are going through a period of change and your guides want you to get ready to shift and adapt quickly.

420: Angel Number 420 appears when your spirit guides want you to take notice of what you are doing to keep your feet on the ground. You want to make sure you are not depending on too many people or things to keep you grounded because then you can be moved by their energy at any moment.

421: Angel Number 421 appears in your life when your spirit guides want you to increase your confidence in a relationship or friendship. You need to remember what you bring to the table and your worth.

***422:** Angel Number 422* appears to let you know that your hard work is not in vain. You are doing an amazing job and will receive a payout for your time and effort really soon. Keep going, people are seeing your hard work and dedication.

***423:** Angel Number 423* appears when your spirit guides want you to know that you are a divine being. You were made in the image of the higher power and must believe and act as such at this time in your life. Others know your power and will feed off your insecurities if you do not see it yourself.

***424:** Angel Number 424* appears when your energy is needed to help create a safe space for yourself and others around you. There is someone who looks up to you and sees you as someone they can depend on. You are very valuable and divinely protected.

***425:** Angel Number 425* appears when your spirit guides want you to know that it's ok to let your child-like self to come out and play. You may have been being very serious lately and your guides want you to laugh and enjoy life more to create true balance.

***426:** Angel Number 426* appears when your spirit guides are calling for you to create proper boundaries in your relationships in order to protect your energy. There may be someone who is depending too much on you and needs to learn how to trust themselves more.

***427:** Angel Number 427* appears when your spirit guides want you to look at the reality of a relationship you are involved in. Is there something you are refusing to take notice or pay attention to? Make sure you are paying attention to the tangible and not imagining what is not there.

***428:** Angel Number 428* appears when your spirit guides want you to know that we all make mistakes in life and you are no different. The things you have gone through from childhood into adulthood have all been integral in who you are today. Allow yourself to embrace the mistakes and transmute them into something you can have authority over.

429: Angel Number 429 appears in your life when your spirit guides want you to understand that nothing lasts forever and all beginnings must have an end. The sooner you find peace in an ending, a new beginning will appear in front of your eyes.

430: Angel Number 430 appears in your life when your spirit guides want you to provide forgiveness for someone whom you feel doesn't deserve it. They want you to remember that the forgiveness is for you and not them. You don't have to ever speak to them again but you don't need your heart to harden.

431: Angel Number 431 appears when your spirit guides are asking you to allow yourself to enjoy the fruits of your labor. You have been working a lot and it is time for you to take some time for yourself and enjoy it.

432: Angel Number 432 appears in your life when you are being asked to remain hopeful about a connection in your life. It may be going through a confusing patch, but that is because you both have been growing and evolving. It's time to acknowledge you all's evolved selves and redefine your needs in the connection.

433: Angel Number 433 appears in your life when your spirit guides are asking you to embrace your feminine energy more. The more in touch with your feminine side that you become, the more peace you will have in your home and working spaces.

434: Angel Number 434 appears when your spirit guides want you to be serious about protecting your projects, investments, and creative energy. Protect them like they are a newborn baby until you are completely ready to release it to the world (if ever).

435: Angel Number 435 appears when your spirit guides are asking for you to spend some time honoring the feminine energies in your life that have had a hand in raising you. This is a perfect time to pay homage because without them, there would be no you.

436: Angel Number 436 appears when your spirit guides want you to be more selective of who you allow around you in your inner circle. You are only as strong as the weakest link and it's important to keep strong links (relationships) and not the fickle ones.

437: Angel Number 437 appears when your spirit guides want for you to be open to new ways of viewing or seeing life around you. You want to make sure you are not being one-track minded to the point you miss out on a great opportunity because it doesn't look like your normal choices.

438: Angel Number 438 appears when your spirit guides want you to remember that you are the main character of your world. At the end of the day you say who or what has access to you. It is time for you to start using that authority.

439: Angel Number 439 shows up when your spirit guides want you to remember that you are growing everyday. Everyday, make sure you are learning something new and applying it to your life when applicable.

440: Angel Number 440 shows up when your spirit guides want you to know that you have access to divine protection, guidance, and support when you need it. There is an unlimited supply available and time of day doesn't matter. Make your petition clear and watch things unfold as long as you believe.

441: Angel Number 441 appears when you are being warned of some potential trickery around you. It is important for you to be aware of your surroundings and the things people are saying to you. Make sure it is applicable to you before taking the advice.

442: Angel Number 442 appears when your spirit guides want you to start connecting with people who have training in mental health support. You are going through a phase in your life when you are learning how to work through and address your personal trauma and it would be helpful to have someone help you work through it.

443: Angel Number 443 appears when you are being called to become more self-sufficient and not depend on others too much, especially feminine energies. It is time to leave the nest and allow yourself to fly.

444: Angel Number 444 appears when your spirit guides want you to know that you are on the right track. You have created the proper boundaries in your life and they are keeping you protected, on task, and grounded. You are walking in wholeness and in the right direction.

445: Angel Number 445 appears when your spirit guides want you to allow your imagination to lead you into this next phase of your life. Things are changing around you and you need to understand how to embrace it fully with an open-minded childlike energy.

446: Angel Number 446 shows up when your spirit guides want you to take notice of the processes you currently use in your life. A simple change in your processing or organization of day to day activities can increase productivity.

447: Angel Number 447 shows up when you are being called to protect your brain and memory. If you have been forgetting things lately or want to protect your memory, start researching brain friendly foods, vitamins, and herbs to help with day to day clarity and memory.

448: Angel Number 448 shows up when you are in the middle of someone else's drama. Your spirit guides want you to remember that it is not your problem and you have to let them solve their problems on their own.

449: Angel Number 449 shows up when your spirit guides are asking for you to be ok with getting rid of things that no longer serve you. There may be some old clothes or items that carry a negative energy that you are refusing to let go of. It is time.

450: Angel Number 450 appears when your spirit guides want you to trust yourself more. Someone may be trying to make you feel guilty about a natural character trait you have that allows you more freedom. Understand their feelings are more so out of jealousy and not true concern. Keep allowing yourself the freedom you deserve.

451: Angel Number 451 shows up when your spirit guides want you to remember that you are in charge of your life and no one else. What you deem to be important is important. What you want to spend your time on is your decision and no one else's. Look within more than outside.

452: Angel Number 452 shows up when your spirit guides want you to know that others are motivated by your youthful energy. They may not tell you, but you provide them with hope that there are still genuine people in the world. Keep showing up authentically you, you are motivating others.

453: Angel Number 453 shows up when your spirit guides want you to not let others' perceptions of you cloud your judgment and future actions. Before taking them seriously, make sure to look at their life and how they are living. Never take advice from someone who isn't happy within themselves.

454: Angel Number 454 appears when your spirit guides sense your need for a change in your life. Things may have been feeling like a bit of a routine and you could benefit from some random changes or fun. Do something that you wouldn't normally do!

455: Angel Number 455 appears when an energy around you is trying to trigger you. Watch out for passive microaggressions from people who are trying to trick you into doing something that would benefit them in the end. They feel you are easily manipulated, but that is not the true case. Do not prove them right.

456: Angel Number 456 shows up in your life when your spirit guides want you to know that you are in direct alignment with abundance. You are being set up for new opportunities and experiences that will teach you valuable lessons for a lifetime.

457: Angel Number 457 appears in your life when your guides are calling for you to release an old way of thinking or approach towards change. Embrace the changes happening in your life and alchemizing the energy for your benefit.

458: Angel Number 458 appears in your life when your spirit guides would like for you to take your control back from others. There is someone who you have allowed to control your space and decisions. It's time to reclaim your authority over your life.

459: Angel Number 459 appears when your spirit guides are asking you to stop trying to stop an endi from happening. This ending will have a big impact on your life in a good way. Allow it to happen, similar to growing pains from going from teenager to adult. Let it happen.

460: Angel Number 460 appears when you are being called to find security in the structures you have placed in your life. You are safe and protected and your guides want you to always remember that nothing has access to hurt you unless you accept it.

461: Angel Number 461 shows up in your life when your spirit guides are calling for you to hand over your worries and cares to them. Let your petitions be known and watch it all unfold. Life is working in your favor.

462: Angel Number 462 shows up in your life when you are called to invite someone into your space to brainstorm out an idea together. This is something you want to bring to life and your guides are bringing someone who is the perfect fit into your space.

463: Angel Number 463 sends a message of hope from your spirit guides. They want you to know that you are walking into an abundant period of your life and it is important that you use proper gatekeeping of your personal space. Only those in alignment with your divine purpose should be granted entry.

464: Angel Number 464 appears in your life when your spirit guides are preparing you for abundance. This abundance will come in the form of new employment or a spiritual raise of some sort. Make sure you are paying your tithes to the universal energy as it comes back to you tenfold.

465: Angel Number 465 shows up when your spirit guides want you to be thankful for the good energy you have around you. This good energy has a lot to do with the abundance and wealth you are attracting. Give thanks.

466: Angel Number 466 shows up to let you know that there is someone around you who is your biggest fan in your face and behind your back. If you have been wondering if you have real people in your circle, your guides want you to know that you have pure souls around you.

467: Angel Number 467 appears when your spirit guides want for you to balance your intuition and knowledge. Sometimes intuition is supreme and sometimes your knowledge is what's important. Know when to use both.

468: Angel Number 468 appears when your spirit guides want you to take more accountability for the actions you have taken to lead you to where you are right now. As you take honest accountability you will be able to move forward without feeling as if you are a victim in all situations.

469: Angel Number 469 is an angel number that appears when your spirit guides are preparing to reward you for sticking to the plan that was set forth for you. You are going through a spiritual graduation.

470: Angel Number 470 sends a reminder from your spirit guides to remember that there is nothing wrong with you. You are perfectly made and only those who vibrate on the same frequency as you will be able to understand you and stick around for the long haul.

471: Angel Number 471 is calling for you to research new things to do with your beauty and self-presentation. How you present yourself to the world is an indication of how you either feel inside or are manifesting.

472: Angel Number 472 shows up when your spirit guides want you to learn new ways to be supportive of others around you. It's important that you show up for others the same way you want them to show up for you.

473: Angel Number 473 shows up when your spirit guides would like for you to learn about your family history. There is something interesting in your family tree that your spirit guides want you to learn about and change in order to create generational blessings.

474: Angel Number 474 appears when your spirit guides are calling for you to stand firm on what you know to be true. You are walking into a period where many will try to make you question yourself and you will have to stand firm on your experience, knowledge, and personal instincts.

475: Angel Number 475 reveals itself when you are ready to jump into a new dimension of time and space. You may have been dreaming and daydreaming more often lately and this is a sign that your spirit is becoming more free and able to roam across spaces that the physical eye can't understand.

476: Angel Number 476 sends a message from your spirit guides to keep proper boundaries in your friendships. Always remember, this is your journey and most times people give advice from their personal experience. Know how to decipher what is for you and what isn't.

477: Angel Number 477 sends a warning from your spirit guides of watching out for distractions at this time. You have been really focused on your work and learning a new skill, which can sometimes attract energies that go against it. Keep firm and know when a space is not safe for you.

478: Angel Number 478 sends a message of protection from any harm. A tower moment may have recently happened or is happening right now around you. Whatever you do, protect your good energy and now that all endings are for your good at the end of the day. A way is being cleared for you to walk through.

479: Angel Number 479 appears when your spirit guides are calling for you to take a spiritual retreat away for your mental, physical, spiritual and emotional health. This time away will give you extended power you have been praying and hoping for.

480: Angel Number 480 shows up when your guides are asking for you to use your authority to make something happen. You were born with an innate skill of leadership and should trust your judgment even in unknown circumstances.

481: Angel Number 481 appears when your spirit guides want you to trust yourself more. You recently made a decision that was best for you and it is important to not let any outside energies interfere with your decision to try and bring guilt.

482: Angel Number 482 appears when your spirit guides want you to connect with other leaders who can help you get stronger in your skills of confidence and communication skills. This change will open your eyes to new horizons and opportunities.

483: Angel Number 483 shows up when your spirit guides are calling for you to communicate effectively with others who are under your leadership. Speak from a place of confidence and be open to hearing their feedback as well.

484: Angel Number 484 appears in your life when it is time to make an executive decision that will benefit the collective energy of people around you. Your spirit guides want you to know that humility will be important, but know what you know to be true at the same time.

485: Angel Number 485 appears in your life when you are craving more freedom in your life. Your spirit guides are calling for you to something sporadic that you have always wanted to do, with no fear!

486: Angel Number 486 appears when your spirit guides want you to know that your hard work is paying off for you! You have entered a period of stability with either your home, finances, health, or work (or even all of them!). Give yourself more credit. Your self-determination is beyond great.

487: Angel Number 487 appears when your spirit guides are calling for you to learn a new skill, no matter how novice it may appear. It could be something such as learning how to ride a bike or swim. Whatever it is, allow yourself the freedom of learning something you always wanted to do.

488: Angel Number 488 appears in your life when your spirit guides would like for you to not allow the disbelief of others to discredit your amazingness. Just because they can't see it, doesn't mean you don't have it!

489: Angel Number 489 appears when your spirit guides are calling for you to step outside of your comfort zone and move on to something new. You have outgrown the space you are currently in and it's time to expand yourself. How can you allow your creative energy to shine?

490: Angel Number 490 appears when your spirit guides want you to leave your space of comfort and jump into an unknown space or endeavor. You will never know what is out there if you don't try. You can always go back again.

491: Angel Number 491 appears when your spirit guides want you to be inspired by what is to come in the near future. Everything is working out for your good and your spirit guides want you to embrace every piece of endings and new beginnings!

492: Angel Number 492 appears when your spirit guides are calling for you to see the beauty in endings you have recently experienced. The endings came as a way to allow you space to keep growing and getting in alignment with your divine soul purpose.

493: Angel Number 493 appears when you are being called to transmute endings in your life into new beginnings. Is there a way you can turn a moment of pain into purpose?

494: Angel Number 494 appears when your spirit guides want you to know that you are in the flow of prosperity from the universe. Negative thinking and endings had to be removed in order for the alignment to happen. A period of stagnation is over.

***495:** Angel Number 495* appears when the wheel of fortune is turning in your favor after a period of intense changes and endings. The cycle of life continues and you are on top right now. Enjoy and embrace it as much as you can.

***496:** Angel Number 496* appears when your spirit guides want you to know that there is no life or living without endings as that is the only constant. Use the endings as a way to navigate in creating new routines to adjust.

***497:** Angel Number 497* appears after a shake-up to your foundation or stability. Your spirit guides sent this number to you to remind you that there is a lesson in everything that happens in your life. Learn from your mistakes and endings so it doesn't become a repeating cycle.

***498:** Angel Number 498* shows up in your life when you are at a place of regaining stability after a period of loss or stagnation. This time is integral in you growing as a person and taking back control of your life.

***499:** Angel Number 499* appears in your life when you are ready to move to a new location, city, or home. Your current space is no longer fulfilling your spiritual and emotional self and it is time to allow something you once depended on to end so the chapter can be closed.

Chapter 7: Angel Numbers 500-599

500: Angel Number 500 is a message from your spirit guides of caution when making changes in your life right now. Anything can happen and you want to make sure you have a deep understanding of all potential outcomes first.

501: Angel Number 501 is a message from your spirit guides to allow your childlike faith to guide you into unknown territory. You are learning a new version of yourself and your spirit guides want you to embrace your quirky uniqueness.

502: Angel Number 502 is a message from your spirit guides to let you know that it is best to just enjoy the moments you have with loved ones in your life without any restrictions and expectations. It will make the experience more worthwhile and enjoyable.

503: Angel Number 503 is a message from your spirit guides to allow yourself freedom to express your creativity in whatever way you want. This is not the time to put restrictions where you will benefit most from child-like freedom and faith.

504: Angel Number 504 is a message from your spirit guides to allow yourself to be open to something that is not like your usual option when it comes to your home, foundation or stability. This is a good time to change up the energy in your home and do something different.

505: Angel Number 505 is a message from your spirit guides to let go of expectations for your life and let it all flow. You may be trying to force yourself into a box that you were never supposed to be in. If your spirit doesn't feel free, you're not supposed to be there.

506: Angel Number 506 is a message from your spirit guides to change your current schedule and allow time to play freely. It is important to plan breaks in you day to day tasks because it keeps your energy free to roam and bring about opportunities you never know existed before.

507: Angel Number 507 is a message from your spirit guides to have fun while you are working and learning new things. When you are having fun it doesn't feel like work. You will find yourself catching on easier by doing this.

508: Angel Number 508 is a message from your spirit guides to have a little fun while taking care of business. Just because you have responsibilities doesn't mean you can't enjoy what you are doing. This is a reminder to not take everything so seriously.

509: Angel Number 509 is a message from your spirit guides to be open to change and actually embrace endings as they mean a new beautiful beginning is enroute to you at the time.

510: Angel Number 510 is a message from your spirit guides to embrace this new you that you have been walking into. This is a new process for you, so they want you to know that you have the ability to define this moment however you choose. The power is yours and you will be supported.

511: Angel Number 511 is a message from your spirit guides to step out on faith and make a change that will benefit you and your purpose. This change should increase your confidence and provide more personal freedom.

512: Angel Number 512 is a message from your spirit guides informing you that it is time to change something about yourself and how you define your freedom in your relationships and connections. You want to make sure you are not losing yourself for the sake of compromise.

513: Angel Number 513 is a message from your spirit guides to make sure you are voicing your needs clearly to others around you. What is the purpose of connections if you aren't comfortable speaking up for yourself?

514: Angel Number 514 is a message from your spirit guides to make a change in your life that will positively impact your stability. By taking the initiative, you are telling the universe that it can help you now.

515: Angel Number 515 is a message from your spirit guides to remind you to never let your child-like faith die out. It is that side of you that makes changes easier to understand because you remain optimistic. Optimism is your friend at this time and your freedom is key.

516: Angel Number 516 is a message from your spirit guides to make sure you are not neglecting your imagination. When you block out limitations in your mind you will see more options appear in your reality.

517: Angel Number 517 is a message from your spirit guides calling for you to make a difficult decision based on new information you have received. It appears difficult now, but will make much more sense in the future when everything stabilizes.

518: Angel Number 518 is a message from your spirit guides to not take yourself too seriously in your daily work. You will find your work life more enjoyable when you stop placing limitations on it.

519: Angel Number 519 is a message from your spirit guides to all facets of your life. Each phase of your life was important for you to be in this moment today so there is no reason to be embarrassed by anything of your past. It is the past that nurtured you into the person you are now.

520: Angel Number 520 is a message from your spirit guides asking you to have more fun with your connections. You may currently have unrealistic expectations of someone based on your personal story, but it's important to learn what is best for them from their version of themselves as well.

521: Angel Number 521 is a message from your spirit guides to be hopeful for a new beginning you have been hoping for in your life. Whether with a person or opportunity in general, your guides want you to stay hopeful when it happens.

522: Angel Number 522 is a message from your spirit guides asking for you to keep your connections and relationships lighthearted at this time. You never know what someone is going through around you and all they need is good energy.

523: Angel Number 523 is a message from your spirit guides letting you know that you bring hope to others at this time. Your kind and youthful spirit gives others permission to be more creative and open about themselves without judgment.

524: Angel Number 524 is a message from your spirit guides suggesting a change in scenery for you. You may have been spending a lot of time in the house and your guides want you to go outside and connect with other people and new activities.

525: Angel Number 525 is a message from your spirit guides encouraging you to connect with others who share the same passion and excitement for life as you. You are in a phase of your life where you are allowing your soul to be free and you deserve to be surrounded by other good energy. Keep embracing the good of life and watch more good changes come for you.

526: Angel Number 526 is a message from your spirit guides encouraging you to connect with someone else to help you navigate your current responsibilities in an orderly fashion to ensure you are making the most of your time and energy.

527: Angel Number 527 is a message from your spirit guides reminding you that there is so much out in the world that you have yet to explore and learn about. The more you experience the greater your internal instinct becomes over time. It's time to expand your knowledge and approach learning from a freedom perspective.

528: Angel Number 528 is a message from your spirit guides letting you know that the universe has granted you grace for mistakes made in the past. You are not being punished for things of the past and its ok to move on into the future now.

529: Angel Number 529 is a message from your spirit guides reminding you that endings are setups for a new beginning. You are being called to allow yourself to bloom into your next season. It's ok to make new friends and do different things now, you are expanding your circle.

530: Angel Number 530 is a message you receive from your spirit guides when they want you to allow your imagination to roam and take you to higher places. You are being called to let your inner-child come out and express yourself creatively. It will open random doors for you that you would have never imagined!

531: Angel Number 531 is a message from your spirit guides asking for you to change a perception you have been holding about yourself that is outdated. You have evolved into a new version of you and do not deserve to be held to old standards that no longer resonate.

532: Angel Number 532 is a message from your spirit guides asking you to shift a perception you have of someone else and how you may think they see you. If they haven't told you something, then it's not fair to assume unless there is concrete evidence. Allow a safe space for others to be themselves and the same will be provided for you.

533: Angel Number 533 is a message from your spirit guides encouraging you to allow your inner child out to play. You are in a powerful manifesting period of your life and the more creative and open-minded you are, the more beautiful life becomes. You are creating the life you have always envisioned.

534: Angel Number 534 is a message from your spirit guides calling for you to accept what makes you stand out from the crowd. This is not the time to compare yourself to others or try to be like someone else. You were born to be you, one of a kind. Stay grounded in that.

535: Angel Number 535 is a message from your spirit guides letting you know that you are called to practice strength in a life changing situation right now. Trust that you will make the right decision from a place of internal intuition. It is important to look at this time of change from a positive perspective.

536: Angel Number 536 is a message from your spirit guides asking you to change your perception of your current life processes and schedules at this time. There is a time and place for everything and this moment in life won't last forever, it's creating a sense of discipline that is needed when you have more freedom of movement.

537: Angel Number 537 is a message from your spirit guides that show up when they want you to take some time to learn something new that will be beneficial for a project you are currently working on or planning to do.

538: Angel Number 538 appears in your life when your spirit guides are asking for you to change your view of leadership. You may have been looking at something from a place of disgust or limitation when everything is subjective to whatever you want it to be for you.

539: Angel Number 539 is a message from your spirit guides telling you that it is safe for you to let go of something that you have been trying to keep a strong grip on. You will notice when you allow more freedom it becomes easier to manage and more fulfilling.

540: Angel Number 540 is a message from your spirit guides that appear when you are being called to create more freedom in your home life and responsibilities. You may have been trying to act one particular way when you are being called to engage in a more individualized way that is best for you.

541: Angel Number 541 is a message from your spirit guides that appears when you are being called to have more grace for yourself at this time. Grace for yourself is important when you are living in a world that lacks it.

542: Angel Number 542 is a message from your spirit guides to embrace your psychic abilities at this time. You may have been having many moments of Deja Vu where you feel like you have experienced something before.

543: Angel Number 543 is a message from your spirit guides to slow down and get your footing at this time. You have a few things that are calling for your focus and you need to have stable grounding in order to work through them with precision.

544: Angel Number 544 is a message from your spirit guides calling for you to be inspired by how far you have come in life. It is important to take this time to be grateful for growth and give yourself a pat on the back for not giving up.

545: Angel Number 545 is a message from your spirit guides to accept your wild and fun side. It is all a part of you and deserves to be acknowledged just like your calm side. This is a reminder to define what stability means for you because it won't look like everyone else's.

546: Angel Number 546 is a message from your spirit guides letting you know that recent changes you've made to your surroundings are attracting a more positive energy to you. Everything you have been doing with intention is working for your good.

547: Angel Number 547 is a message from your spirit guides to never stop dreaming and learning new things. The more you know, the better decisions you make. The better your decisions, the more positive manifestations enter your space!

548: Angel Number 548 is a message from your spirit guides to have grace for yourself and your status. You may have been feeling swamped by everything and your guides want you to take a breath and give yourself some slack. You're doing great!

549: Angel Number 549 is a message from your spirit guides letting you know that a recent change you made is bringing an ending that was inevitable. Whatever is unable to meet your high frequency no longer has a place in your energy so celebrate the ending.

***550:** Angel Number 550* is a message from your spirit guides that shows up when they want for you to explore your life with no boundaries. You are in a period of your life when you will benefit more when you allow your inner free spirit to roam and embrace even the smallest of things around you.

***551:** Angel Number 551* is a message from your spirit guides to trust what you feel more than what you see. Eventually how you feel will match your outer reality as the vibration continues to shift so will your actions which creates a ripple effect.

***552:** Angel Number 552* is a message from your spirit guides to allow grace to someone around you who is going through a difficult time right now. They may be acting out due to their personal issues. This is not saying to accept their behavior, but allow this to be a teaching moment for the next time you encounter someone in a similar situation.

***553:** Angel Number 553* is a message from your spirit guides letting you know that it is time to accept a new way of thinking when it comes to your personal freedom. Where have you been holding yourself back due to fear? It's time to take your power back and live.

***554:** Angel Number 554* is a message from your spirit guides to forgive yourself for not being able to show up for others the way they expected you to. You are not like everyone else and if no one else understands... at least allow yourself the grace to understand yourself.

***555:** Angel Number 555* arrives in your life when your spirit guides want you to gear up for your life to be changed dramatically, in a good way! You are being called to take a leap of faith towards something that makes your heart feel free with no limitations. You are destined to be successful!

***556:** Angel Number 556* is a message from your spirit guides to change your routine to fit your life schedule better. Make sure you are allowing time for fun and self-care in the midst of the busyness.

557: **Angel Number 557** is a message from your spirit guides informing you that changes are coming soon that you will have to use your natural instincts to navigate. Use your past knowledge to make the best decision.

558: **Angel Number 558** is a message from your spirit guides that it is time to increase your personal confidence in yourself. Whatever you do, do not compare yourself to anyone else and use this time to identify what makes you uniquely amazing.

559: **Angel Number 559** is a message from your spirit guides to let go of control and allow things to happen the way it needs to happen. You may have been trying to hold onto things and people that need to be let go of. Let the natural order happen.

560: **Angel Number 560** is a message from your spirit guides informing you to keep some space available in your daily schedule that allows flexibility in the case something else comes up that you want to attend to.

561: **Angel Number 561** is a message from your spirit guides to take a new course of action towards a goal you have set for yourself. Go in with positive energy and expect to see its success as you work towards it.

562: **Angel Number 562** is a message from your spirit guides to embrace new concepts and creative ways to teach it to others. You will find great success in your new way of delivery.

563: **Angel Number 563** is a message from your spirit guides informing you to protect your innocent positive energetic nature at all costs because unhappy negative energies will not like seeing you vibrate higher. It's not your problem at the end of the day.

564: **Angel Number 564** is a message from your spirit guides letting you know that you are favored from the universe and are protected from any negative energies or wishes of harm. Your energy is stronger than any hate.

565: Angel Number 565 is a message from your spirit guides asking for you to learn from past experiences you have gone through. Forgive yourself for anything you are not proud of and transmute it into something different.

566: Angel Number 566 is a message from your spirit guides asking for you to step into your divinity at this time. You are going through a spiritual transformation and a key part is learning that you are divine.

567: Angel Number 567 is a message from your spirit guides letting you know that the grace you have offered yourself has opened doors for you to attract increased protection over your health and positive energy. You are stepping into a new season of your life.

568: Angel Number 568 is a message from your spirit guides asking for you to protect your natural characteristics that others may try to demonize. You were made perfectly and possess something in you that no one else can duplicate.

569: Angel Number 569 is a message from your spirit guides letting you know that it is time to be the change that you want to see in the world. You will see others in your energy begin to follow your lead.

570: Angel Number 570 is a message from your spirit guides telling you that it is important to keep an open mind with new information you have been receiving lately. Do not push something away because it is unfamiliar, you just may need it in the future.

571: Angel Number 571 is a message from your spirit guides reminding you that you have the power to attract luck to you in whatever way you decide. You just need to make sure you are intentional.

572: Angel Number 572 is a message from your spirit guides letting you know that it is time to take an assessment of who and what you have around you. If they are not in alignment with what you are manifesting, you need to readjust the time and energy given to the connection.

573: Angel Number 573 is a message from your spirit guides informing you of incoming communication from someone who you haven't heard from in a long time, but will be excited to hear from. You will get some interesting ideas from talking to them.

574: Angel Number 574 sends a message from your spirit guides informing you that others are learning from you whether you see it or not. They have been observing how you move and how you talk. Keep being you.

575: Angel Number 575 is a message from your spirit guides calling for you to be optimistic about the direction your life is headed. Be excited for the abundant wealth you are attracting due to your increased confidence of self.

576: Angel Number 576 is a message from your spirit guides encouraging you to not have too many boundaries placed over your work life and manifestations. Boundaries limit how and when you receive it.

577: Angel Number 577 is a message from your spirit guides letting you know that the changes you have made have opened the door for luck and abundance to enter your life. You are in a great space spiritually and energetically.

578: Angel Number 578 is a message from your spirit guides letting you know that it is time to make an executive judgment on the direction you will be moving in. You may be playing more than one side (juggling) and you are being called to choose which way you will be moving in, with confidence.

579: Angel Number 579 is a message from your spirit guides letting you know that as soon as you apply new information you have recently received, you will begin to see immediate results in your beauty, confidence, and creativity.

580: *Angel Number 580* is a message from your spirit guides telling you to keep your faith in the future. Even when you can't see the end of the staircase, know that you are headed in the right direction as long as you are being obedient to yourself.

581: *Angel Number 581* is a message from your spirit guides informing you that it is time to change how you have been protecting your energy from the outside world. If you have been noticing mood swings or shifts lately, this is your reminder to check and clear your energy field.

582: *Angel Number 582* is a message from your spirit guides letting you know that you have an addictive energy to you that others can't explain. You are very influential and there is someone who loves seeing you show up and shine your light.

583: *Angel Number 583* is a message from your spirit guides to keep pushing towards your goals. Your hard work is paying off and it's important for you to award yourself the same grace that you give others.

584: *Angel Number 584* shows up when your spirit guides want you to remember why you made the decision to do something. This is your reminder to stay up to date with your feelings to make sure you always remember your "why" in order to keep going.

585: *Angel Number 585* appears in your life when your spirit guides are preparing you for a level up in life. You are being called to be open to the changes and have grace for yourself as you learn the new skill that will be required of you.

586: *Angel Number 586* is a message from your spirit guides to learn a new way of handling your day to day business dealings. Your old routine may be outdated and you're being called to adjust.

587: *Angel Number 587* is a message from your spirit guides informing you that it is time for you to start putting more energy into your spiritual self. As you invest more into your spiritual side, it will spill over into other areas of your life positively.

588: Angel Number 588 is a message from your spirit guides telling you that it is important that you accept all sides of yourself and do not try to hide from the world. Even the side of yourself that once embarrassed you have a purpose for you. Use it for your benefit.

589: Angel Number 589 is a message from your spirit guides to change how you approach change in your life. When things need to end, it's best to accept it as a blessing and opportunity to create something new.

590: Angel Number 590 brings a message of divine change in your life. Things may seem unpredictable at this time which is not bad like it may seem at first glance. You are being divinely guided into an unknown space that will bring good energy.

591: Angel Number 591 is a message from your spirit guides pushing you into a new beginning after learning something new about yourself that you hadn't been aware of before.

592: Angel Number 592 is a message from your spirit guides to allow yourself to sit with yourself in order to get back into alignment with your complete self. You may have been running on fumes lately and need to recharge yourself.

593: Angel Number 593 is a message from your spirit guides telling you that there is something blocking your creativity and manifesting power at this time. Whatever doesn't allow with your open-mindedness and child-like faith to roam free needs to go.

594: Angel Number 594 is a message from your spirit guides calling for you to have compassion for someone in your life who is having a hard time adjusting to changes in their life. They are not asking you to physically interfere, but send positive energy their way as they work through it.

595:Angel Number 595 is a message from your spirit guides to enjoy the current changes and endings happening in your life right now. It is all about the journey more than the destination. You are going through a divine period of your life right now as you remove parts of your old self.

596: Angel Number 596 appears in our life when you are being stretched to see how far your limits go. This period of your life is teaching you your inner strength to show you what you are able to manage. This period of your life is teaching you your boundaries.

597: Angel Number 597 is a message from your spirit guides letting you know that it is time to let go of old ways of thinking that no longer serve you and the direction you are going in life. It is hurting you more than helping.

598: Angel Number 598 carries messages from your spirit guides informing you of your royal authority on earth and in the spirit world. You are a divine being and hold great authority within your voice and energy to those around you.

599: Angel Number 599 is here to let you know that change is inevitable and it is best to embrace it with excitement for what's to come versus fight it. You will enjoy life much more when you do.

Chapter 8: Angel Numbers 600-699

600: Angel Number 600 is a message from your spirit guides letting you know that it is best to have flexibility in your life right now. You never know what may happen and when you would need to move around.

601: Angel Number 601 is a message from your spirit guides letting you know that everything you want is currently manifesting in your life because you are doing the work.

602: Angel Number 602 shows up when you are about to receive divine favor to help with current projects you are working on.

603: Angel Number 603 is a message from your spirit guides letting you know that communication is key when it comes to getting what you want and need. When you are honest you will know who or what is best for you.

604: Angel Number 604 is a message from your spirit guides that appears when you are completing a karmic cycle that is not serving you. Life will begin to feel more abundant soon.

605: Angel Number 605 is a message from your spirit guides to schedule fun into your life if you have to. Without fun and some freedom, life begins to get a little boring and uneventful. You have to create the excitement you want.

606: Angel Number 606 is a message from your spirit guides telling you that what goes up will always have to come back down. It is best to always tell the truth in situations you are faced with. If you don't, it will come back to bite you.

607: Angel Number 607 is a message from your spirit guides suggesting you make sure you are protecting your intellectual property from energies that want to steal and not give your credit when due.

608: Angel Number 608 is a message from your spirit guides letting you know that if you want a particular life, you need to create the space for it now as if it was already here.

609: Angel Number 609 is a message from your spirit guides that show up to tell you that any closed door was never really the door for you. What is meant for you will happen without reservation.

610: Angel Number 610 is a message from your spirit guides letting you know that how you treat yourself is how the world will view your worth. You have been doing a great job of showing others how to treat you, whether you see the fruits of it or not.

611: Angel Number 611 is a message from your spirit guides to make sure you are protecting yourself and not allowing others to make you into a martyr.

612: Angel Number 612 is a message from your spirit guides that appears when you are being called to share what you have learned with others around you right now. You have acquired great skills that others would benefit from.

613: Angel Number 613 is a message from your spirit guides to protect your creative feminine energy at all costs. You have a skill that is very beneficial to others and the wrong people will try to use it without giving you your flowers.

614: Angel Number 614 is a message from your spirit guides to put more time into how you present yourself to the world. You will notice a difference in the type of attention you receive when you dedicate time to that area.

615: Angel Number 615 is a message from your spirit guides to allow the current organized chaos in your life right now. You are naturally getting everything into flow and the last thing you want to do is limit your potential.

616: Angel Number 616 is a message from your spirit guides to stop talking more than doing at this time. Many won't see your dopeness until they see it manifest in the physical.

617: Angel Number 617 is a message from your spirit guides to not allow anyone into your space that has not proven their worthiness. You run the risk of attracting users at this time, who don't bring mutual benefit.

618: Angel Number 618 is a message from your spirit guides to take what you have learned from the past and incorporate it into your present moment.

619: Angel Number 619 is a message from your spirit guides letting you know that it would be smart to make more decisions that benefit you and your personal needs at this time.

620: Angel Number 620 is a message from your spirit guides to take action towards an idea you have been wanting to test. Even if it doesn't go the way you want, it will provide the opportunity to learn something new that will benefit in the future.

621: Angel Number 621 is a message from your spirit guides to get prepared for a new beginning that will be happening in your life soon. You have been prepared for this moment.

622: Angel Number 622 is a message from your spirit guides to research potential opportunities and partnerships that will work with your current situation.

623: Angel Number 623 is a message from your spirit guides to organize some time with those closest to you like your family or friends. Time with them will rejuvenate your energy and give you good energy.

624: Angel Number 624 is a message from your spirit guides calling for you to take the steps towards making something known around you. It is ok to judge things and people around you to make sure they are in alignment with you.

625: Angel Number 625 is a message from your spirit guides calling for you to tap into your natural instincts. Your natural instincts will let you know when you are in a safe space or not.

626: Angel Number 626 is a message from your spirit guides telling you to stay the course and remain focused on your goals. Your schedule and organization plays a key role in your productivity.

627: Angel Number 627 is a message from your spirit guides telling you to protect your space and move smart. If your intuition tells you a space or person isn't safe; trust it the first time.

628: Angel Number 628 is a message from your spirit guides to not share too much about yourself with others around you right now. You need to feel out a space before jumping in head first.

629: Angel Number 629 is a message from your spirit guides asking for you to get prepared for an ending that is approaching. This is something you have known was coming to an end for quite some time and your guides want you to gear up for the finale.

630: Angel Number 630 is a message from your spirit guides asking for you to let yourself be guided by love and everything that is meant for you will cling to you. Those who aren't will be rattled by your spirit.

631: Angel Number 631 is a message from your spirit guides asking for you to pay more attention to yourself for a while. You have been quite busy and need to take some time for yourself.

632: Angel Number 632 is a message from your spirit guides asking for you to pay more attention to the most important connection in your life right now. Are you taking out time to nurture those relationships?

633: Angel Number 633 is a message from your spirit guides letting you know that you manifest more fun, excitement, and joy when you have a collective or friend group to bask in the good energy with at this time in your life.

634: Angel Number 634 is a message from your spirit guides reminding you that your words have intense power and you want to make sure you are speaking what you want to manifest into existence.

635: Angel Number 635 is a message from your spirit guides asking you to drop your schedule for the day and allow your inner child to guide you and do whatever it tells you to (nothing illegal though lol)

636: Angel Number 636 is a message from your spirit guides letting you know that you are increasing your productivity by focusing on the parts of yourself that keep you healthy and able to thrive. Your health is getting better.

637: Angel Number 637 is a message from your spirit guides letting you know that your good energy is attracting random luck. You will find people are happier and giving to you at this time.

638: Angel Number 638 is a message from your spirit guides asking for you to take some time to nurture your divine feminine energy. When you let your feminine be free, it will guide you to make the best decisions for yourself.

639: Angel Number 639 is a message from your spirit guides calling for you to take things out of your daily routine that do not benefit you in the long-run. It is important to reserve your energy for what and who matters most.

640: Angel Number 640 is a message from your spirit guides letting you know the importance of having a foundation before jumping into something. If you jump too soon, you won't be grounded enough to sustain it.

641: Angel Number 641 is a message from your spirit guides cautioning you to pay attention to who or what you are getting your advice from. Make sure they are in alignment with your soul and where you are headed.

642: Angel Number 642 is a message from your spirit guides that shows up when your guides are calling for you to incorporate others into your daily life more, especially if you have been in hermit mode. Healthy human connection is beneficial.

643: Angel Number 643 is a message from your spirit guides that appear when they are calling for you to protect your stability and good energy. You are vibrating higher than many people around you right now and your guides want you to be protective of who has direct contact and access.

644: Angel Number 644 is a message from your spirit guides when they are calling for you to focus more on your mental and physical health at this time. You are only as strong as your health is and it's time to make some healthy choices. Make that a priority at this time.

645: Angel Number 645 is a message from your spirit guides letting you know that alot of things around you are changing and it's important for you to not get too attached to the tangible things around you right now.

646: Angel Number 646 is a message from your spirit guides when they want you to remember that you are love and the love inside of you is what will continue to sustain you, especially in moments of doubt, fear, or confusion.

647: Angel Number 647 is a message from your spirit guides letting you know that many of the best things in life are free. Everything isn't about how much something costs or the name attached to it.

648: Angel Number 648 is a message from your spirit guides asking for you to take a look at your upbringing for clues on what is going on now in your life and how to make needed changes.

649: Angel Number 649 is a message from your spirit guides that appears when you are outgrowing a current situation or place in your life. Your spirit guides are asking you to take an inventory of the space around you to make sure it is still of a beneficial nature to your development.

650: Angel Number 650 is a message from your spirit guides suggesting that you uncover truths that have been hidden from you in plain sight. You will find yourself seeing things from a different perspective when you take off rose-colored frames.

651: Angel Number 651 is a message from your spirit guides suggesting that you look within yourself to see what it is you love about yourself before wondering if others love you. You are the first one to define that about yourself.

652: Angel Number 652 is a message from your spirit guides letting you know that recent changes that have happened in your life were meant to happen in order to bring more stability into your life and space. Change comes in many forms.

653: Angel Number 653 is a message from your spirit guides asking for you to not give up on yourself or your dreams. They can and will come true as long as you continue believing in yourself and keeping your child-like faith.

654: Angel Number 654 is a message from your spirit guides to not give up on a dream you have for yourself. Whatever you do, just make sure you are grounded and have an outlined process to guide how you will accomplish it. If you don't, it's time to create a plan.

655: Angel Number 655 is a message from your spirit guides that appears when they want you to make some adjustments to the plan you had laid out for your life. Sometimes plans change OR the path you take to get there changes. Either way it goes, it's ok to pivot.

656: Angel Number 656 is a message from your spirit guides letting you know that no matter what you do, you will be protected in the spiritual world and physically. It's ok to want freedom and stability at the same time. This is your world and you are the main character of your story.

657: Angel Number 657 is a message from your spirit guides asking for you to let go of anything that no longer serves you in the new energy you are in now. As you forgive yourself and others you find it easier to accept the endings as they are needed for a new beginning.

658: Angel Number 658 is a message from your spirit guides asking for you to take control of your mental health at this time. Any anxiety or stress you have been experiencing can be transmuted into hope through intention. Replace the behaviors you don't want with healthier alternatives. When you are intentional, and receive proper support, nothing is too hard for you.

659: Angel Number 659 is a message from your spirit guides letting you know it is time to slow down and allow your body to rest. You have been moving around alot and this has had an impact on your physical health. More rest increases your brain cognitive functioning.

660: Angel Number 660 is a message from your spirit guides letting you know that it is important to know how to encourage yourself in times when you need it. Someone else will not always be there to support you, so it's best to incorporate other methods to support you when needed.

661: Angel Number 661 is a message from your spirit guides that appears when you are in alignment mentally and spiritually, but spirit wants you to focus on your physical. Make sure what you are consuming is good for your health long-term.

662: Angel Number 662 is a message from your spirit guides about resiliency. You are very resilient and nothing is too hard for you when you put your mind to it. Keep going, change is over the horizon.

663: Angel Number 663 is a message from your spirit guides reminding you that sometimes people don't take you seriously until you show them what you mean by withdrawing. It is time to stop talking and trying to convince someone of something and just lead by example. It's not your job to convince anyone of anything.

664: Angel Number 664 is a message from your spirit guides letting you know that you are creating a blessing you have spoken into existence. You are using what you have learned to create better opportunities.

665: Angel Number 665 is a message from your spirit guides letting you know that your plans are protected from any harm or destruction at this time. You will be called to change a few things but it will be for your benefit.

666: Angel Number 666 is a message from your spirit guides letting you know that you are a carbon copy and there is no one else like you around. There may even be people trying to duplicate things that you do as a way to attract good things in their life. Keep showing up as an example.

667: Angel Number 667 is a message from your spirit guides letting you know that you are going to be put into the spotlight for something that you are doing right now. Keep moving with integrity and good energy.

668: Angel Number 668 is a message from your spirit guides letting you know that you are living a good life as long as that's how you define good. You have allowed yourself to experience a multitude of things in order to find what is best for you and you are being rewarded for it.

669: Angel Number 669 is a message from your spirit guides calling for you to find the lesson in the changes that have been happening lately in your life. You have the power to change how it affects your mood and it is best to use it to your advantage.

670: Angel Number 670 is a message from your spirit guides that shows up when they want you to research new holistic ways to manage your mental health needs at this time. You do not want to get dependent on substances that are hard to break away from when needed.

671: Angel Number 671 is a message from your spirit guides asking for you to be aware of changing truths around you. It is important to make sure you are not operating off outdated beliefs or information. It's time to do an update on your personal knowledge about something important in your life.

672: Angel Number 672 is a message from your spirit guides that appears when they want you to pay attention to your morning routine at this time. How you start your day is how your day will go as the time passes. Start it as how you want to feel, think, and do.

673: Angel Number 673 is a message from your spirit guides that show up when they want you to take notice of the changing feelings of people around you. It is important to take an inventory of those closest to you and see if you are showing up how they may need you right now.

674: Angel Number 674 is a message from your spirit guides reminding you that it is best to not question life, but to become an active participant in what happens. You are not a victim, but a creator. Take things as they are and create what you want from it.

675: Angel Number 675 is a message from your spirit guides reminding you that nothing happens by coincidence. An ending that recently happened was actually setting you up for something greater. You will always be taken care of and provided for, do not fret.

676: Angel Number 676 is a message from your spirit guides for you to take an inventory of how strong you really are. You may have been downplaying your strength and your guides want you to take a look at what life has taught you thus far and protect the innocence you have acquired over time.

677: Angel Number 677 is a message from your spirit guides asking for you to align your passion with your day to day life. You may want a particular thing but your life doesn't reflect those things you want.

678: Angel Number 678 is a message from your spirit guides letting you know that the steps you have been taking have given you relevant information to guide you into becoming the main character of your life. This is a warning that as you walk more into your divinity, those who are not will begin to fall away.

***678**: **Angel Number 678** is a message from your spirit guides letting you know that the steps you have been taking have given you relevant information to guide you into becoming the main character of your life. This is a warning that as you walk more into your divinity, those who are not will begin to fall away.

***679**: **Angel Number 679** is a message from your spirit guides to accept that which you have not control over and focus on the things you can control. This will preserve your energy for what really needs it.

***680**: **Angel Number 680** is a message from your spirit guides for you to get in touch with your inner boss and identify what makes you stand out in the world. There are things you have inside of you that others do not. Use those skills as your "wild cards" in life.

***681**: **Angel Number 681** is a message from your spirit guides informing you that your current positions in life are protected at this time. There is no need to worry about anyone affecting your stability or progress.

***682**: **Angel Number 682** is a message from your spirit guides letting you know that you will be coming into contact with another person walking in their personal truth. Find a way for you both to co-exist without feeling as if you are stepping on each other's toes. Everyone has their own strengths and weaknesses.

683: **Angel Number 683** is a message from your spirit guides that appears when you may be getting tired of the mundane aspects of life. You may feel like wanting to run away from your responsibilities and this is a reminder that it's ok to take breaks every now and then. It may be time to take one and not beat yourself up about it.

***684**: **Angel Number 684** is a message from your spirit guides reminding you that you are an attraction magnet. When you chase opportunities they elude you. Become the vibe of what you want to attract and allow it to happen in its time.

685: ***Angel Number 685*** is a message from your spirit guides to open your schedule up for the next week or so. Change something up about it and do something that you don't normally do. You will find it to be a benefit to your brain function and excitement for life. Life isn't supposed to feel boring and mundane.

686: ***Angel Number 686*** is a message from your spirit guides letting you know that as your mental and physical health get stronger so will your confidence in self and your personal authority in the world. You are a divine being in this earthly plane and it is important to treat yourself like royalty.

687: ***Angel Number 687*** is a message from your spirit guides informing you to double check any information being shared with you at this time. You want to make sure it aligns with your authentic self and the direction you are intentionally walking into.

688: ***Angel Number 688*** is a message from your spirit guides letting you know that it is important to make sure the life you live is matching the life you speak. It is easy to judge others for things that trigger us, when in reality it is meant to be a reality check to let you know where there are cracks in the foundation.

689: ***Angel Number 689*** is a message from your spirit guides letting you know that you may need to forgive yourself for a mistake that you have recently made and are still beating yourself up for. On this earth, you will make mistakes and it is important to forgive yourself and keep moving forward.

690: ***Angel Number 690*** is a message from your spirit guides letting you know that something in your daily routine is changing or needs to be changed in order to open yourself up for more opportunities.

691: ***Angel Number 691*** is a message from your spirit guides reminding you that the universe is always helping you reach your personal goals. You can expect divine guidance to be received in an unexpected way in the next 7 days.

***692:** Angel Number 692* is a message from your spirit guides reminding you to remember why you chose to let something or something go in your life, before you make the decision of letting it back into your life. Never allow what hurt you back in for another chance to hurt you again.

***693:** Angel Number 693* is a message from your spirit guides letting you know that you are walking into a new creative period of life after a harsh ending of some sort. This will make up for anything that was lost.

***694:** Angel Number 694* is a message from your spirit guides letting you know that you are transitioning into a new energy that brings stability and abundance after a time of loss and deprivation. Keep going, you are walking in the right direction.

***695:** Angel Number 695* is a message from your spirit guides when they want you to remain hopeful for what can happen in your future. Life is not linear and the energy you put in is the energy you receive through your personal perception. It's time to have fun with both the ups and downs of life and watch things continue getting better.

***696:** Angel Number 696* is a message from your spirit guides when they are asking for you to find a healthy replacement for any behaviors you have been changing. By doing this, you are allowing yourself to create new habits that are beneficial to you.

***697:** Angel Number 697* is a message from your spirit guides that appears when they want you to make sure you are not being too arrogant at this time with nothing to back it up. It is best to notice it and humble yourself before someone else attempts to.

***698:** Angel Number 698* is a message from your spirit guides informing you to only get involved in situations that involve you and your personal development. Someone may be trying to get you involved in their personal life problems and it has nothing to do with you. This is a lesson that was given to them for a reason.

***699:** Angel Number 699* is a message from your spirit guides that appears when your guides want to congratulate you for putting new actions, behaviors, and structures in place in order to attract the energy you do want into your life. It is all paying off.

Chapter 9: Angel Numbers 700-799

700: Angel Number 700 is a message from your spirit guides asking for you to take some time away from the familiar and seek out something new that you have never learned about before.

701: Angel Number 701 is a message from your spirit guides asking for you to jump into the unknown and try something new that you have always wanted to do for yourself.

702: Angel Number 702 is a message from your spirit guides letting you know that anything can happen between you and another person so it's important for you to remove any type of expectations that you are holding.

703: Angel Number 703 is a message from your spirit guides that appears when you are being called to look into new creative endeavors or opportunities that allow you to express yourself more freely.

704: Angel Number 704 is a message from your spirit guides calling for you to get your financial affairs in order before making any important decisions that require you to spend money.

705: Angel Number 705 is a message from your spirit guides that appear when you feel you are going through a difficult time expressing your free spirit. You are being called to create a safe space for you instead of trying to find one at this time.

706: Angel Number 706 is a message from your spirit guides that appears when you are being called to protect your energy as you go through a transition. You are very impressionable and don't want to have the wrong influences around you.

707: Angel Number 707 is a message from your spirit guides that appear when you need to remember that knowledge is the key to true freedom in the world. As you learn more, it is important to protect yourself from vultures who don't want the same.

708: Angel Number 708 is a message from your spirit guides to protect your personal space. You are the main character of your home and the last thing you need is the wrong energy in your space which then transfers to other areas of your life.

709: Angel Number 709 is a message from your spirit guides when they want you to know that a difficult financial situation is coming to an end and abundance is right about the corner. Make sure you are a good steward of what you are given.

710: Angel Number 710 is a message from your spirit guides letting you know that a moment you have been waiting for, is finally here! Something has been completed and you are about to start seeing things moving forward in your favor.

711: Angel Number 711 is a message from your spirit guides asking for you to fact check everything before taking information and running with it and putting it into action. A piece of information may be misconstrued.

712: Angel Number 712 is a message from your spirit guides that appear when they feel you are ready to share something that you recently learned with someone else. They will be grateful for your support and knowledge.

713: Angel Number 713 is a message from your spirit guides calling for you to find a new way to monetize a creative gift you have been cultivating for some time.

714: Angel Number 714 is a message from your spirit guides that appears when you are being called to embrace your spiritual side more. You may have been acting more out of analytical brain waves when you are called to embrace your intuitive side more.

715: Angel Number 715 is a message from your spirit guides that is calling for you to remove some of the boundaries you have placed on yourself, which has been limiting you from reaching your full potential.

716: Angel Number 716 is a message from your spirit guides encouraging you to go out and be what it is you feel others have neglected to be for you. You are called to be the hero in your own story now.

717: Angel Number 717 is a message from your spirit guides that appears when you need to be reminded that you have divine knowledge that needs to be protected and secured inside of you in preparation for a windfall of abundance enroute of you.

718: Angel Number 718 is a message from your spirit guides that shows up when you are walking in divine favor. You are a walking abundance magnet and the more confident you are, internally, the more you attract externally.

719: Angel Number 719 is a message from your spirit guides asking you to define what abundance means to you and reject everything else. You may have recently been comparing your needs to others and it hasn't been a positive outcome.

720: Angel Number 720 is a message from your spirit guides when they want for you to connect with other people who are in alignment with you intellectually and spiritually. You will benefit from intellectual conversations at this time.

721: Angel Number 721 is a message from your spirit guides asking for you to remove yourself from the critiques of others and define who you are from your own perspective.

722: Angel Number 722 is a message from your spirit guides that reveals itself to you when you are ready to receive information from an outside source to help you increase intellectual knowledge and status in the spiritual world. You will be given new esoteric knowledge that everyone isn't privy to receiving.

723: Angel Number 723 is a message from your spirit guides calling for you to take a serious look at your personal beliefs and figure out if they are limiting you or giving you freedom of choice and self. You may be holding on to outdated beliefs that are no longer true for your soul.

724: Angel Number 724 is a message from your spirit guides to think before you engage with others right now. When you do engage, make sure you are grounded in how you approach them and have a well-defined reason why.

725: Angel Number 725 is a message from your spirit guides that appear when you are called to connect with your inner child and information you learned when you were younger but fell away from. You will find by connecting with this side of freedom more abundance is attracted to you.

726: Angel Number 726 is a message from your spirit guides to balance and categorize new information you are receiving right now. By organizing everything, it will make it easier to process through it all.

727: Angel Number 727 is a message from your spirit guides calling for you to protect your intellectual property at this time. You embody a great deal of information that is valuable when it is in the wrong hands. You are a protector of esoteric information, and only other chosen ones should be given access to it. You will know when it's right.

728: Angel Number 728 is a message from your spirit guides that arrive when you are being called to use wisdom and grounded judgment with how you present yourself to others, especially new people in your circle. You may need to be a master of disguise for a while to peep out the scene first.

729: Angel Number 729 is a message from your spirit guides letting you know that you have a piece of knowledge that could bring a destructive institution crumbling down if you wanted it to. Use what you know wisely because you can bring a tower at any moment.

723: **Angel Number 723** is a message from your spirit guides calling for you to take a serious look at your personal beliefs and figure out if they are limiting you or giving you freedom of choice and self. You may be holding on to outdated beliefs that are no longer true for your soul.

724: **Angel Number 724** is a message from your spirit guides to think before you engage with others right now. When you do engage, make sure you are grounded in how you approach them and have a well-defined reason why.

725: **Angel Number 725** is a message from your spirit guides that appear when you are called to connect with your inner child and information you learned when you were younger but fell away from. You will find by connecting with this side of freedom more abundance is attracted to you.

726: **Angel Number 726** is a message from your spirit guides to balance and categorize new information you are receiving right now. By organizing everything, it will make it easier to process through it all.

727: **Angel Number 727** is a message from your spirit guides calling for you to protect your intellectual property at this time. You embody a great deal of information that is valuable when it is in the wrong hands. You are a protector of esoteric information, and only other chosen ones should be given access to it. You will know when it's right.

728: **Angel Number 728** is a message from your spirit guides that arrive when you are being called to use wisdom and grounded judgment with how you present yourself to others, especially new people in your circle. You may need to be a master of disguise for a while to peep out the scene first.

729: **Angel Number 729** is a message from your spirit guides letting you know that you have a piece of knowledge that could bring a destructive institution crumbling down if you wanted it to. Use what you know wisely because you can bring a tower at any moment.

730: Angel Number 730 is a message from your spirit guides letting you know that you are very intelligent and capable of finding out how to profit from the knowledge and creative gifts you possess. Allow yourself to sit and brainstorm what and how to do it.

731: Angel Number 731 is a message from your spirit guides that arrive when you are in a fertile energy to start something new based off past experiences or research you have done. Be excited about what is to come!

732: Angel Number 732 is a message from your spirit guides reminding you that nothing is impossible to complete when your heart and dedication is in it. You are a magician and have strength and power in your words. Speak it and bring it all into reality!

733: Angel Number 733 is a message from your spirit guides when you are in a strong manifesting period of your life. Your words are very powerful and it's important to have a strong control over your words and thoughts!

734: Angel Number 734 is a message from your spirit guides calling for you to speak life over your home. When was the last time you did a cleanse over your space? It just may be time for you to clear out stagnant energy to make room for positive movement.

735: Angel Number 735 is a message from your spirit guides that arrives when you are called to use what you have learned over the years to create the freedom you have been praying for. You are a master creator!

736: Angel Number 736 is a message from your spirit guides letting you know its time to organize your abundance that has been coming to you. You have an abundance of knowledge, energy, support, and more finances coming your way!

737: Angel Number 737 is a message from your spirit guides calling for you to protect your creative freedom at this time. You have a particular approach to manifesting your desires through your work and someone may be trying to alter your perception of what you are doing and how. Keep following your purpose.

738: Angel Number 738 is a message from your spirit guides calling for you to be increase your personal confidence and be excited for all the things currently happening in your life and everything that is enroute to you!

739: Angel Number 739 is a message from your spirit guides to allow yourself to elevate spiritually. You have recently learned new information that challenges your old perceptions of the world. Allow it to happen and stop fighting it.

740: Angel Number 740 is a message from your spirit guides when they want you to take a moment and look around you at all of the blessings you already have. You have an unlimited amount of abundance within you and you can have it wherever you decide to go.

741: Angel Number 741 is a message from your spirit guides letting you know that your sense of confidence and self is motivating to others who are starting something that you are seen as a veteran at.

742: Angel Number 742 is a message from your spirit guides letting you know that it is safe to share information with someone in your space that you recently met. It is not too good to be true, you both were brought into each other's life for a divine purpose of friendship and connection.

743: Angel Number 743 sends a message from your spirit guides relating to finding peace in your journey. You have come a long way to get to where you are right now and it's important to have moments of reflection to see just how you experiences have been more of a benefit than not.

744 Angel Number 744 is a message from your spirit guides asking for you to not take anything that someone else does personally. You have to remember that we are all here on this journey to become our best selves and sometimes you will be collateral damage in someone else's story just as some are in yours as well. Understand, forgive and move on.

745: Angel Number 745 is a message from your spirit guides to allow yourself the freedom to choose what is best for you. You may be still holding yourself back due to boundaries created from someone else in your life.

746: Angel Number 746 is a message from your spirit guides informing you that you are picking up popularity with people around you. They are talking about your resiliency and how you never stay down for too long. You are a motivation to many, keep living your life your way.

747: Angel Number 747 is a message from your spirit guides calling for you to ground yourself in your personal beliefs. What do you believe when it comes to the knowledge you have acquired? How have your personal instincts grown over time? What about your spirituality? This is a good time to sit with yourself to identify what you really believe at this point in your life.

748: Angel Number 748 is a message from your spirit guides calling for you to approach a situation from a grounded perspective. You may have to put your foot down about something or to hold someone accountable. You want to approach them from a place where they will understand so don't do it while you are fuming angry or in the heat of feelings.

749: Angel Number 749 is a message from your spirit guides letting you know that you are elevating to a higher level with your earthly assignment. You have been raising your vibration and things that are at a lower vibration level no longer resonate with you.

750: Angel Number 750 is a message from your spirit guides calling for you to change your approach to how you share your knowledge with the world. Others may not see things how you do and when you share things in spaces where they are not welcoming to it, you will be met with resistance.

751: Angel Number 751 is a message from your spirit guides calling for you to go inside yourself and set yourself free from the boundaries you have been placing on yourself from thoughts of others. It's important for you to define yourself before you let someone else do it for you.

752: Angel Number 752 is a message from your spirit guides encouraging you to free your mind and free yourself from anyone who is unable to accept who you have become. This is your life journey and you deserve the right to be free with how you live it.

753: Angel Number 753 is a message from your spirit guides reminding you that your mind is the biggest investment you will ever make in this lifetime. Protect it at all costs, but not so much that you fear being free. Just keep your energy cleansed and pure to keep anything not worthy of your energy away.

754: Angel Number 754 is a message from your spirit guides calling for you to recognize the power you hold in the spaces around you. You may have been selling yourself short while others see you as a powerhouse. Look up, not down.

755: Angel Number 755 is a message from your spirit guides to remind you that you are exactly where you need to be. This is not the time to think about who or what is no longer here with you. Who needs to be around you, are and that is all that matters.

756: Angel Number 756 is a message from your spirit guides asking for you to look around you to see how lucky you are. You have overcome a lot in your life and this is only the beginning of your story. Keep going and continue writing it your way.

757: Angel Number 757 is a message from your spirit guides letting you know to never let go of your child-like energy you embody inside of you. This energy is what will set you free in the future, enabling you to move at the beat of your own drum. Keep going.

758: Angel Number 758 is a message from your spirit guides when they feel it is time for you to upgrade yourself from student to teacher. You have spent quite a bit of time learning a new skill and getting in-tune with yourself and you are ready to start sharing with the world.

759: Angel Number 759 is a message from your spirit guides that appears when you have officially let go of old ways of thinking and are moving into the next phase of your life. It was the grace you extended yourself in unknown times that helped you the most.

760: Angel Number 760 is a message from your spirit guides to protect your space while you open yourself up to the unknown at this time. You are in a vulnerable state and its important to keep away from manipulators or energy vampires.

761: Angel Number 761 is a message from your spirit guides that appears when you are preparing to enter a new career or are being called to look into researching new career options that are more promising for your educational advancement, growth, and financial increase.

762: Angel Number 762 is a message from your spirit guides that appears to let you know that it is ok to trust the psychic feelings you have been experiencing lately. Your gifts are increasing as you tap more into your feminine energy.

763: Angel Number 763 is a message from your spirit guides informing that people are watching your life questioning why and where your blessings are coming from. Watch out for new people coming into your energy trying to glean from your vibrations without any reciprocity.

764: Angel Number 764 is a message from your spirit guides reminding you to not only protect your energy, but know when something is not worth the energy it takes to create. Preservation of your energy is imperative at this time.

765: Angel Number 765 is a message from your spirit guides asking you to take inventory of any behaviors you may be engaging in to keep from facing reality at this time. Make sure you are not masking yourself behind things to keep from working through uncomfortable feelings or thoughts.

***766:** Angel Number 766* is a message from your spirit guides letting you know that you have people in your life who want to see you win. Some of them are unable to support you publicly but they are sending you positive messages energetically. All of your guardian angels won't be seen. Focus and connect with good energy.

***767:** Angel Number 767* is a message from your spirit guides letting you know that when you are working on your life purpose everyday won't be an easy one, but it will be worth it. It is important to have processes in place to support you when you find yourself wanting to question your purpose and journey. You are on track, keep going.

***768:** Angel Number 768* is a message from your spirit guides letting you know that your hard work and dedication has not been in vain. You are manifesting your dreams and it will come in due time. Just keep getting prepared, learning new ways to express yourself, and keep positive spirits.

***769:** Angel Number 769* is a message from your spirit guides calling for you to keep strong boundaries around you as you keep elevating your energy. There will be times when people will try to put their heavy weight on you when they feel you can take it. Don't let them trauma dump on you because you appear abundant in good energy. Stop them at the door.

***770:** Angel Number 770* is a message from your spirit guides to get ready to evolve into the next phase of your life spiritually, mentally, and knowledge wise. You are doing an amazing job. Keep elevating!

***771:** Angel Number 771* is a message from your spirit guides to pay attention to your brain mental capacity at this time. You do not want to overload your brain with too much at one time. Slow down and let it happen. It will all flow in the way it is supposed to.

***772:** Angel Number 772* is a message from your spirit guides to move with confidence at this time. Your intuitive gifts are increasing whether you have been trying to tap into them or not. They are here because you have been getting stronger in your divine feminine energy and that is a result of allowing the energy to roam without restrictions. Embrace this new phase.

773: Angel Number 773 is a message from your spirit guides asking you to connect more with your feminine energy. The more intune you are with your feminine energy, the more creative and intuitive you will become because you are in alignment with mother earth's divine energy.

774: Angel Number 774 is a message from your spirit guides letting you know that you are being elevated to a higher level of status. You are being viewed as a wise individual to others and you will find more people coming to you for advice and learn from you.

775: Angel Number 775 is a message from your spirit guides letting you know that this may not be the best time to put too much pressure on others or trust them to show up when you need them. You are being called to become more self-sufficient on your own energy at this time.

776: Angel Number 776 is a message from your spirit guides telling you that it is ok to not know what is happening or what is coming next. Allow yourself to remain curious, this is what makes you a lifelong learner.

777: Angel Number 777 is a message from your spirit guides letting you know that you have entered a lucky period in your life right now. Allow yourself to receive what is coming your way in your communications, connections, and financial wealth. Your creativity is above average and you are being called to start acting on it full blown!

778: Angel Number 778 is a message from your spirit guides calling for you to travel outside of yourself to learn about a new culture or topic you have never explored before. There is a piece of information that is valuable for your level-up.

779: Angel Number 779 is a message from your spirit guides letting you know that you are not going crazy, you have just outgrown your current situations. When you increase your awareness, knowledge, and vibrations, energies that don't align start to try and work against you to keep you stuck. It's time to move on from something or someone.

780: Angel Number 780 is a message from your spirit guides letting you know that it is time to take your skills to another level! You will never know how successful you will be if you don't at least jump out there and try!

781: Angel Number 781 is a message from your spirit guides informing you that recent steps you have taken are pushing you into increased knowledge and confidence that no one will be able to take from you. Keep your hand close to you for a little while longer.

782: Angel Number 782 is a message from your spirit guides informing you that justice is yours at this time. You standing up for yourself and holding your ground is causing others to get karma for things they intentionally did to you. Revenge is not for you to take. Let nature run its course when someone hurts you. It's best to let life take care of it.

783: Angel Number 783 is a message from your spirit guides letting you know that a tower moment is currently happening around you. This tower moment is a manifestation of something that has happened in the past. Whether it is your tower or someone else's, know that it isn't an indication of worth, yet a reminder that everything we do, has a consequence whether good or bad.

784: Angel Number 784 is a message from your spirit guides calling for you to keep your mind strong at this time. You are walking into a point of your life where your leadership or decisions may be questioned by people who are trying to doubt you. Do not pay them any attention. Your job is not to convince others, yet to just live as yourself as an example of light.

785: Angel Number 785 is a message from your spirit guides calling for you to be the inspiration that you are seeking from other people at this time. You have a lot of natural wisdom in you from personal experience and innate wisdom that you were born with. Trust it.

786: Angel Number 786 is a message from your spirit guides telling you it is time to step out on faith in an area of your life. You may have been feeling smothered or controlled and feel the strong urge for freedom. This angel number is saying your energy is not trying to confuse you, it wants you to see your value and understand that your current work environment is no longer a healthy place for you to grow.

787: Angel Number 787 is a message from your spirit guides telling you to trust the decisions you have made in your recent past. You have made decisions that are best for you, your mental health, stability, and spiritual self. You are walking into a time of spiritual abundance and favor.

788: Angel Number 788 is a message from your spirit guides when they feel you have been working really hard and deserve a break. It's time to make some time for your closest loved ones, turn off your work mind, and have some fun!

789: Angel Number 789 is a message from your spirit guides letting you know that you are walking as a highly favored high priestess! Everything you touch and speak about turns to gold. You speak life into others and manifest easily so make sure you're only speaking those things you desire.

790: Angel Number 790 is a message from your spirit guides asking for you to slow down on making decisions based solely off what is tangible or what makes sense. Just because something doesn't make sense doesn't mean it's not the right thing.

791: Angel Number 791 is a message from your spirit guides when they want you to allow yourself to dream a little. You don't have to always be serious and its ok to dream about the what-ifs.

792: Angel Number 792 is a message from your spirit guides letting you know that you are about to come into union with someone else who is on a similar journey. Your time of feeling lonely is coming to an end.

793: Angel Number 793 is a message from your spirit guides that shows up when you are being called to have more compassion for yourself and others. This is a reminder that you are in a web of spiritual beings having a human experience.

794: Angel Number 794 is a message from your spirit guides letting you know that as you increase your knowledge and understanding of the world around you, certain things will no longer resonate with you. When that happens, don't fight it and seek out new energies to connect with that do align.

795: Angel Number 795 is a message from your spirit guides calling for you to allow your mind to roam free at this time. Let go of any inhibitions and take a leap of faith!

796: Angel Number 796 is a message from your spirit guides letting you know that a divine change is underway. You don't see it right now, but it is on its way to you because you have been manifesting this. When it happens, do not feel confused; it was always meant to be.

797: Angel Number 797 is a message from your spirit guides telling you that you are ending a period of not understanding what was happening in your life. You had to be removed from spaces that were not allowing you to learn or grow before something else happened. You are being called into a higher domain at this time.

798: Angel Number 798 is a message from your spirit guides letting you know that the wheel of fortune is falling into your lap. This is because you have stayed positive and hopeful in the midst of chaos and this is your reward.

799: Angel Number 799 is a message from your spirit guides letting you know that you are entering a period of your life when you are called to teach other what you have come to learn. You are ready!

Chapter 10: Angel Numbers 800-899

800: Angel Number 800 is a message from your spirit guides letting you know that there are many things you have yet to learn and experience in the world. Keep an open mind as you start to uncover hidden details about life that you could've ever imagined.

801: Angel Number 801 is a message from your spirit guides calling for you to take charge of your life. You may have been trying to live by someone else's rules and it's time for you to live by your own. Say no to what you don't want to really say yes to.

802: Angel Number 802 is a message from your spirit guides letting you know that you will never know what will happen if you don't try. You could be introduced to a whole new world by doing one thing.

803: Angel Number 803 is a message from your spirit guides that shows up when you are called to take a creative approach to how you manifest in life. Do not be afraid to tap into parts of yourself that you normally try to hide.

804: Angel Number 804 is a message from your spirit guides reminding you that security is subjective and you have the ability to create the life you want to live. Take the risks and make it happen.

805: Angel Number 805 is a message from your spirit guides that appears when you are going to unknown changes and growing pains in your life. Even though you may not understand how and why it's happening, your guides want you to know that it's for your best.

806: Angel Number 806 is a message from your spirit guides calling for you to put proper precautions in place to protect yourself and your possessions from being overtaken by something or someone else. This isn't the time to be too trusting with strangers.

807: Angel Number 807 is a message from your spirit guides that arrive when they want you to be open to the unknown world and all that it holds. There is so much for you to learn and everything you are taking in right now will benefit your physical, mental, and spiritual health.

808: Angel Number 808 is a message from your spirit guides that show up when you are manifesting unlimited knowledge, abundance, and energy. This is an integral part of your journey so make sure you are taking advantage of all opportunities.

809: Angel Number 809 is a message from your spirit guides calling for you to embrace the unlimited possibilities and opportunities available to you at this time. Remain hopeful and let any fear dissipate.

810: Angel Number 810 is a message from your spirit guides calling for you to make sure you do not lose yourself in the midst of handling responsibilities you have with others.

811: Angel Number 811 is a message from your spirit guides to embrace the power you have and use it to your advantage with no regrets. When you put yourself at this time, you will find yourself being more productive with forward movement.

812: Angel Number 812 is a message from your spirit guides to take a risk that you have been wanting to do for a long time. It's time to initiate your curiosity and allow it to guide you into a new domain that will eventually lead you to what you have been seeking.

813: Angel Number 813 is a message from your spirit guides letting you know that you are manifesting through your creative energy at this time. There is a hidden skill that you have yet to explore that will bring you great abundance.

814: Angel Number 814 is a message from your spirit guides to put something into place to ensure the safety and protection of your homes and valuables. You need to protect yourself from the unknown and things that can potentially happen. This is a preparation energy.

815: *Angel Number 815* is a message from your spirit guides letting you know that it is time to take action towards a change you have been contemplating for some time. The sooner you make the change, the sooner your mood will shift into a happier one.

816: *Angel Number 816* is a message from your spirit guides calling for you to embrace the current laws and restrictions in place. As you respect them, you realize they are in place for you to prosper. You just need to learn how to work with them versus against them.

817: *Angel Number 817* is a message from your spirit guides letting you know that your words have power. When you speak, people listen to you so make sure you are understanding and using that authority wisely.

818: *Angel Number 818* is a message from your spirit guides letting you know that the actions you take today affect your manifestations tomorrow. So make sure you are in alignment with what you say that you want or it will elude you.

819: *Angel Number 819* is a message from your spirit guides calling for you to not run from endings. Endings are a beautiful opportunity to create the new beginning you want to happen.

820: *Angel Number 820* is a message from your spirit guides to connect with other like minded people who you can network with. You are working on something that takes having a community support. You shouldn't try and do it alone.

821: *Angel Number 821* is a message from your spirit guides letting you know it would be a good idea to delegate roles and responsibilities to others at this time. Especially if you have been busy handling mundane tasks.

822: *Angel Number 822* is a message from your spirit guides that arrive when you have been holding yourself from a certain communication out of fear of being misunderstood. Your voice matters and when you hold back to please everyone, you are left with the brunt end.

823: Angel Number 823 is a message from your spirit guides encouraging you to reconnect with your inner knowing of divinity and sexuality. Not everyone is worthy of your sexual energy. It is best to transmute it through creative pursuits and watch you bring in everything you've been wanting.

824: Angel Number 824 is a message from your spirit guides that show up when you are entering a new period of stability. You can expect a raise or increase in some other way that will allow you to expand.

825: Angel Number 825 is a message from your spirit guides calling for you to show your power without reservation. You are a powerful change agent, but you may be in spaces that aim to keep you feeling small. It's time to explore unknown territory that allow you to bring the fun zest back into your life.

826: Angel Number 826 is a message from your spirit guides asking for you to look inside yourself and ask; Am I living or surviving? It's time to take an assessment to make sure you're not letting life just pass you by.

827: Angel Number 827 is a message from your spirit guides calling for you to apply recent knowledge you have acquired. This newfound knowledge will be integral in a new project you will be in charge of. Believe in the unknown.

828: Angel Number 828 is a message from your spirit guides letting you know that there is a secret someone is keeping from you or you are keeping from someone else. Either way it goes, sometimes privacy is most important until you are sure no one else's energy will affect your manifestations.

829: Angel Number 829 is a message from your spirit guides asking for you to embrace the current healing energy flowing around you. You are being called to balance and allow whatever doesn't heal you to be released.

830: Angel Number 830 is a message from your spirit guides encouraging you to travel to an unknown place. This can be through a book or actual travel. Either way it goes, learning someone else's culture helps you connect better with others.

831: Angel Number 831 is a message from your spirit guides calling for you to stick to the plan you have set for yourself. It's time to allow the talents you have allowed to lay dormant out to play. You will be happy you did!

832: Angel Number 832 is a message from your spirit guides asking for you to share what you have learned with someone else whom you are close to. You have information that could help them with their current situation. Just be creative in how you do it.

833: Angel Number 833 is a message from your spirit guides letting you know that new skills are being developed inside of you and if you don't use them, you will lose them. You are a powerful manifester at this time and it is important to keep your thoughts, pursuits, and self-actions in alignment with what you are desiring.

834: Angel Number 834 is a message from your spirit guides asking for you to document your accounts of a situation in your life. You documenting this now, will enable future generations to be aware of information they wouldn't have had access to previously.

835: Angel Number 835 is a message from your spirit guides letting you know that you have divine favor from above at this time. Use this time to make any adjustments to your crafts because you are about to be put into a spotlight and you want to be confident and comfortable.

836: Angel Number 836 is a message from your spirit guides asking you to be prepared for the unknown. At this time, anything can happen. It is important for you to have an open mind and be ready to take charge where needed. The more structured you are with boundaries the smoother it will be.

837: Angel Number 837 is a message from your spirit guides calling for you to change your perception of history and things that have happened to you in your life. You may be looking from a place of victimhood when your guides want you to see all sides of the situation to form a balanced perspective and perception.

838: Angel Number 838 is a message from your spirit guides to stand firm in your convictions, what you have learned, and experienced. You may be at a time when people want to change you and you are being called to remain true and firm on what you stand for.

839: Angel Number 839 is a message from your spirit guides letting you know that a period of power or leadership may be leaving. Embrace this opportunity and find ways to transform it into a new space of your life. If you didn't learn anything, you have learned the power of creating opportunities after old ones leave.

840: Angel Number 840 is a message from your spirit guides that shows up when you are being called to stand on what you believe. You have gone through a lot to get to this point and only those who are worthy can intertwine with it. You will be breaking barriers in an area that others thought was impossible.

841: Angel Number 841 is a message from your spirit guides letting you know that you are seen as a safe haven for others who feel like they don't have anyone to depend on. Keep being you.

842: Angel Number 842 is a message from your spirit guides that shows up when you are preparing to come into a divine partnership with someone who is stable and grounded just like you. You will be an equal match.

843: Angel Number 843 is a message from your spirit guides letting you know that you are supported from the universe in your creative pursuits and endeavors. Even though you can't see it, know it is there.

844: Angel Number 844 is a message from your spirit guides that shows up when you are being grounded to remember that you are one being in the midst of millions. Spirit wants you to remember that you are special and so are others who are living in their truths.

845: Angel Number 845 is a message from your spirit guides letting you know that you have the power to demand change in a specific area of your life. People see you as a voice of reason and feel you are someone who should be listened to. Use your power and fearlessness to benefit you and others.

846: Angel Number 846 is a message from your spirit guides to keep some things to yourself at this time. Although you know something to be true, it doesn't mean others will be able to accept it just yet. Many around you are still finding their way.

847: Angel Number 847 is a message from your spirit guides to stay connected to someone or something that you are learning from. This person or place is helping you evolve at fast rates whether you see it or not.

848: Angel Number 848 is a message from your spirit guides letting you know that you are manifesting abundance for your household. This has been through you making good informative decisions, staying private, and only connecting with those who are in alignment with you.

849: Angel Number 849 is a message from your spirit guides that shows up when you need to make an executive decision about something in your home life. You may have been ignoring the changes needed to be made, but it is time to make it happen.

850: Angel Number 850 is a message from your spirit guides that show up when you are going through a position shift in your life. This could be a family position or even a job. Either way it goes it will award you more freedom to do what you want.

851: Angel Number 851 is a message from your spirit guides asking for you to get prepared for a change that is coming your way. This change will give you more freedom in your everyday life, so it is safe to embrace it if that's what you desire.

852: Angel Number 852 is a message from your spirit guides asking you to find empowerment in the midst of recent changes in your life. As you assert yourself into different circles you will find your confidence increases.

853: Angel Number 853 is a message from your spirit guides letting you know it is important for you to have grace for yourself and decisions you have recently made in hopes of creating a space where you can be free and abundant. The lessons learned are beneficial for your next steps if you allow it to be a lesson.

854: Angel Number 854 is a message from your spirit guides that appears when they want you to make an executive decision about something that relates to your stability. You have been holding on to something too tightly and it's time to let it loose.

855: Angel Number 855 is a message from your spirit guides that appears when your spirit guides want to remind you that you are a manifestation of the energy you put into the world. Leave behind the energy that is not suiting you and connect with that which is what you desire more of.

856: Angel Number 856 is a message from your spirit guides that appears when you are entering a period of stability that is interchangeable. Whatever you do, remember you are the creator of your life and fate. Your actions taken now will last for years to come.

857: Angel Number 857 is a message from your spirit guides that appears when they are calling for you to establish a stronger relationship with facing the unknown. You may have been afraid of what you can't see, but that can be changed by exploring those things that frighten you at surface level.

858: Angel Number 858 is a message from your spirit guides letting you know that you have always been the conductor of your life and not an outside person or entity. The sooner you grasp this concept and change how you move, you will see a drastic change in your life. Have compassion for yourself as you allow what you used to feel and believe to fall away.

859: Angel Number 859 is a message from your spirit guides that appears to let you know that the recent changes you have made are wiping away everything and everyone who isn't aligned with you anymore. You can trust these changes and those who remain after the sweep.

860: Angel Number 860 is a message from your spirit guides asking for you to remain hopeful for the things the universe has promised to be enroute of you. Everything is working in perfect order and you will continue receiving as you continue the path.

861: Angel Number 861 is a message from your spirit guides letting you know that abundance is available to you in however way you choose to get it. You don't have to follow a certain set of rules, just know you will be held accountable to the energy you accept so choose your path wisely.

862: Angel Number 862 is a message from your spirit guides that shows up when you are being asked to get a handle on your various relationships and responsibilities. There may be a lot going on and a lot of wasted time. You want to make sure you are spending most of your time doing the things you want to do.

863: Angel Number 863 is a message from your spirit guides when they want you to draw attention to how you have been perceiving your current responsibilities. The attitude you have while doing your work also affects its manifestation. If you don't enjoy what you are doing then you shouldn't be doing it.

864: Angel Number 864 is a message from your spirit guides informing you that time is subjective and only matters to those who live on the clock of the world's matrix. You can indeed create your own reality of time when you think about it.

865: Angel Number 865 is a message from your spirit guides letting you know that what you do to others and put your energy into is what you will receive back. Whatever you do and any decisions you make, know that it can potentially happen to you as well so always make conscious decisions.

866: Angel Number 866 is a message from your spirit guides when you are being called to learn how to communicate precisely and with as few words as possible.

867: Angel Number 867 is a message from your spirit guides when you are being called to expand your thinking bigger. You may have been limiting yourself due to lack of knowledge or trust that you could reach higher. Time to stop limiting yourself.

868: Angel Number 868 is a message from your spirit guides for you to protect your time, energy, and space. You may run into others soon who do not know how to respect your energy, time, and space... make sure you keep firm boundaries as they are energy vampires.

869: Angel Number 869 is a message from your spirit guides letting you know that others are watching you take control of your life and are in awe of how you are able to create magic from the lemons life tried to give you.

870: *Angel Number 870* is a message from your spirit guides asking for you to learn from past generations and use what you have learned to influence your future decisions.

871: *Angel Number 871* is a message from your spirit guides asking for you to take action on what you have recently learned about your history. You are a generational blessing creator.

872: *Angel Number 872* is a message from your spirit guides letting you know that they are proud of you and how far you have come. You take a new energy everyday to life and you show up 100% authentically you. Keep going.

873: *Angel Number 873* is a message from your spirit guides calling for you to create something in order to bring information you have gathered to life. You are very fertile at this time in your life so it is important to be intentional with where you put your energy.

874: *Angel Number 874* is a message from your spirit guides asking for you to have unconditional love for yourself and your loved ones at this time. Unconditional love doesn't mean allowing others to continuously hurt you, it means to forgive and understand where they are coming from; even if you have to remove yourself from them.

875: *Angel Number 875* is a message from your spirit guides asking you to switch off your analytical mind and allow yourself to be open to the mysteries of the world.

876: *Angel Number 876* is a message from your spirit guides that are letting you know that you have reached a level of ascension that has unlocked new avenues for you to pursue now that the mental chains have been removed. Your third eye is open and that has now opened new doors of opportunity for you.

877: *Angel Number 877* is a message from your spirit guides calling for you to pay attention to your feminine cycle at this time. As you begin to eat more healing foods, do more healing activities, and remove things that are damaging you will find your cycle syncing with either the new moon or new moon. Once you reach this place, your magic will be 100x stronger!

878: Angel Number 878 is a message from your spirit guides of truth. You have been a seeker of truth and you have landed upon a new discovery in your life right now. Protect what you have learned, everyone is not ready for the information you have received.

879: Angel Number 879 is a message from your spirit guides that appears when your spirit guides are asking for you to leave reality for a moment and dream a little more. Allow your energy to roam as it feels called to, with no restraints. You can always command it back in line.

880: Angel Number 880 is a message from your spirit guides letting you know that you are in a manifestation period where anything is possible. It is important that you use this time to use what you have learned within esoteric knowledge, current life situations, and ancestral knowledge to divine that which you desire.

881: Angel Number 881 is a message from your spirit guides telling you that it is important for you to show up as your biggest fan at this time. There may be others who do not believe in you and want to see you fail. You have to be able to see beyond their smaller perception of you and rise above.

882: Angel Number 882 is a message from your spirit guides encouraging you to allow yourself to find your soul tribe. You may have been in hermit mode after going through a transition. Your spirit guides want you to know that there is a community of people who have experienced something similar and you would be welcomed with open arms.

883: Angel Number 883 is a message from your spirit guides asking for you to look at things from a bigger perspective. You may have been looking at an issue from a micro personal level, when you need to be looking at the larger implications in order to get the full picture and understanding.

884: Angel Number 884 is a message from your spirit guides to encourage yourself when there is no one else around to encourage you. You have the power to be all things and sometimes you only have yourself there to show up for you. This is a reminder that you are the empowerment that you seek from others.

885: Angel Number 885 is a message from your spirit guides to step into the unknown with confidence and be the change you want to see in the world. If there is something that you want to see happen, but it's not created yet. It was waiting for you to create it. Have faith that it will all work out.

886: Angel Number 886 is a message from your spirit guides asking for you to take a look at your life's timelines. You have overcome so much and have the power inside of you to overcome much more as you grow more powerful.

887: Angel Number 887 is a message from your spirit guides asking for you to research rituals to help you increase your confidence in yourself and what you have to offer the world. What is your beauty ritual? What is your confidence ritual? What is your bedtime ritual? It's time to take a new approach to things and become intentional.

888: Angel Number 888 is a message from your spirit guides letting you know that you are in a very powerful manifesting energy. Everything you have been working on, in good energy, is bringing you good karma and your guides want you to keep your magic to yourself while you are in this sensitive energy. Once you have completed this current journey, you can then share with others.

889: Angel Number 889 is a message from your spirit guides letting you know that a karmic cycle has come to an end for you. You have learned alot from the experience and now it's on to the next journey in life.

890: Angel Number 890 is a message from your spirit guides calling for you to let go of the painful karma of your past in order to walk into your new journey. By holding on to the past, you are allowing yourself to stay connected to what brought you pain. You are in an energy of renewal.

891: Angel Number 891 is a message from your spirit guides Congratulating you for taking the necessary steps towards personal transformation that leads to spiritual and emotional fulfillment. The answers have always been inside of you, not outside.

*892: **Angel Number 892*** is a message from your spirit guides to remove any behaviors, actions, or people who do not align with your higher self and purpose.

*893: **Angel Number 893*** is a message from your spirit guides to take control of your intellectual and creative energy. You are not to be controlled but honored and supported for your gifts to this world.

*894: **Angel Number 894*** is a message from your spirit guides reminding you to see the beauty in all things. This helps keep you grounded as you embark on new journeys.

*895: **Angel Number 895*** is a message from your spirit guides to let go of your strong grip and allow yourself to expand without boundaries. Get into the energy of change and watch everything flourish like a seed dropped to the ground by a bird in the sky. Although it was an accident, it still had a beautiful purpose for the person who will watch it grow taller daily.

*896: **Angel Number 896*** is a message from your spirit guides encouraging you to pay more attention to your spiritual needs over your physical needs. When you are elevated spiritually, everything in the physical will align with your vibration.

*897: **Angel Number 897*** is a message from your spirit guides calling for you to use this time as an opportunity for a deep transformation. You are going through a rebirth at this time, embrace every part of it!

*898: **Angel Number 898*** is a message from your spirit guides of hope. No one has the power to move or influence you when you have the proper spiritual and physical boundaries in place.

*899: **Angel Number 899*** is a message from your spirit guides to be like water at this time in your life. It's time to tap into your deep emotional intuitive energy like the depths of the ocean. In the moment of darkness you can be a very strong conduit of energy and flow. Use it the way you wish, you are going through a purification process.

Chapter 11: Angel Numbers 900-999

900: *Angel Number 900* is a message from your spirit guides reminding you that sometimes endings happen unexpectedly and when they do, it's important that you remember that sometimes they happen for no reason at all. This is not a time to take things personally.

901: *Angel Number 901* is a message from your spirit guides letting you know that a recent ending may have caused some confusion but this is a reminder that it was for your best good. Take action to heal from this ending now, while you can still control the energy.

902: *Angel Number 902* is a message from your spirit guides that shows up when they want for you to have compassion for those who you do not understand. You are at a place in your life when you come into contact with a variety of people, try to understand first.

903: *Angel Number 903* is a message from your spirit guides that appears when you are called to have compassion for a group of people who have hurt you or caused you to feel unseen. Empathy may be hard, but anger makes you age faster.

904: *Angel Number 904* is a message from your spirit guides to take a moment and assess your current stability. What have you been doing to get to this point? What has been working and what hasn't?

905: *Angel Number 905* is a message from your spirit guides to have more compassion for the world and how much it has changed over time from how you have known it. It's impossible for things to always stay the same. There will always come a time when we have to adjust to the new way of doing things.

906: Angel Number 906 is a message from your spirit guides to know that you are protected and there is no reason to fear harm or danger. Everything is continuously working out for your good.

907: Angel Number 907 is a message from your spirit guides calling for you to embrace growing up. Growing up is a time of maturation that allows you to collect new information, wisdom, and knowledge that can be bestowed upon the next generation after you.

908: Angel Number 908 is a message from your spirit guides letting you know that you are nearing the end of a period of time where it felt like you had many responsibilities with no understanding of when it would end. You have done an amazing time and things will begin to slow down for you soon.

909: Angel Number 909 is a message from your spirit guides letting you know that you are a powerful alchemist. You have the power to turn the unknown into the known, the weak into someone strong, the sick into the healed, the sad into joyful. You have a way of healing the souls of others through your energy.

910: Angel Number 910 is a message from your spirit guides that shows up when your spirit guides want you to release fear and allow yourself to walk into the unknown world. You will never know until you try.

911: Angel Number 911 is a message from your spirit guides letting you know that you have the power to turn anything around to work for you and your good. You are not a victim to the world, yet you take whatever hurt, pain, or disappointment that may come and turn it around to work for your favor.

912: Angel Number 912 is a message from your spirit guides that appears when they feel you are ready to move on into a new partnership. Whether romantic or platonic, you are being called to allow yourself the opportunity to connect with others again.

913: Angel Number 913 is a message from your spirit guides that appears when you are called to get outside of the house and embrace nature more. By being around nature, you are able to recharge and gain a great balance of self and spirit.

914: Angel Number 914 is a message from your spirit guides that shows up when you are called to have compassion for yourself as you go through a difficult transition at this time. The more compassion you have for yourself and enjoy the process, the more free you will feel spiritually.

915: Angel Number 915 is a message from your spirit guides that appears when you are called to do something that makes your inner child come out and explore the world from a childlike perspective.

916: Angel Number 916 is a message from your spirit guides to change how you protect your energy at this time. You may be in a position where you are around more people, which means you are taking on more at this time. It is time to research stronger ways to protect yourself and your energy from those around you.

917: Angel Number 917 is a message from your spirit guides calling for you to break a generation curse that has been going on in your family for quite some time. You are the chosen one to finally bring it to an end.

918: Angel Number 918 is a message from your spirit guides to embrace your new position either at work, in a group of friends, or your family and home life. You are being seen as a wise individual and others respect your authority.

919: Angel Number 919 is a message from your spirit guides that appears when you are going through a personal transition in your life and you need to make sure you have compassion and patience for yourself as you go through this process.

920: Angel Number 920 is a message from your spirit guides calling for you to test the spirits around you. What this means is, test the people and agencies you are connecting to in order to make sure they are in alignment with your growth spurt you are going through at this time. If not, they need to be released.

921: Angel Number 921 is a message from your spirit guides calling for you to leave something or someone that no longer serves your life purpose behind. The only thing it will do is hold you back from achieving the goal that has been set.

922: Angel Number 922 is a message from your spirit guides letting you know that someone around you has changed their perspective of you and is more understanding of who you are, from a place of compassion.

923: Angel Number 923 is a message from your spirit guides that shows up when you are about to see the manifestation of something you have been working on with a group. This will cause great joy for everyone involved.

924: Angel Number 924 is a message from your spirit guides calling for you to not operate in denial of truth. You may have been running from something out of fear of what it could mean if you embraced it completely.

925: Angel Number 925 is a message from your spirit guides that shows up when you are leaving an old part of your life behind and being joined with something new and exciting. No need to fear or worry, you will be given unlimited grace for any mistakes you make as you make the transition.

926: Angel Number 926 is a message from your spirit guides calling for you to watch out for people who drain your energy. These are energy vampires who only survive by taking energy from other people. With you being such a compassionate person, it makes you a potential victim to them.

927: Angel Number 927 is a message from your spirit guides calling for you to continuously learn about people who are different from you as a way to learn how to best work with them. It is imperative you do this if you want to get through the day to day simpler.

928: Angel Number 928 is a message from your spirit guides that appears when you are being elevated to a new position of authority. Embrace it, you have worked hard for this.

929: Angel Number 929 is a message from your spirit guides that appears when you are going through a transformation in a relationship that is dear to you. This transformation may feel like a difficult ending, but it is only creating an opportunity for elevation for you both.

930: Angel Number 930 is a message from your spirit guides to not take everything at face value at this time. Some things may appear one way right now, but below the surface it is a totally different thing.

931: Angel Number 931 is a message from your spirit guides that appears when you are in a fertile period of your life. It is best for you to take the time to write out what you would like to see happen in your life.

932: Angel Number 932 is a message from your spirit guides to get to the core of an issue that has been ruffling feathers or your stability in an area of your life. It may not be as difficult as it seems, but first you must decipher.

933: Angel Number 933 is a message from your spirit guides asking for you to take an inventory of your friendships and what you share at this time. If a series of interesting events have been happening, it is best to start with who you have been sharing most of your information with.

934: Angel Number 934 is a message from your spirit guides calling for you to be open to trusting again after being betrayed by someone in your life. Eventually you will have to open yourself up to others again, just make sure you are careful this time around.

935: Angel Number 935 is a message from your spirit guides that shows up when they want you to know that you have divine protection around you and they are proud of you for staying hopeful and full of faith while going through unknown situations.

936: Angel Number 936 is a message from your spirit guides to have more compassion for others who think differently from you. It doesn't mean something is wrong with them, they just look at things differently.

937: Angel Number 937 is a message from your spirit guides to evolve from an outdated way of thinking that no longer suits you or your life.

938: Angel Number 938 is a message from your spirit guides that shows up when they want you to change your perception of leadership at this time. As you are able to respect others for their role, you will find the same happening for you when the time comes.

939: Angel Number 939 is a message from your spirit guides that appear when your spirit guides are asking for you to separate yourself from the collective space for a while in hermit mode. This will allow you the opportunity to recharge your mental and emotional health at this time, without distractions.

940: Angel Number 940 is a message from your spirit guides calling for you to work through a current struggle that may be weighing you down. You will be receiving support sooner than you think. Right now, you need to learn to stabilize your feelings in the face of anxiety first.

941: Angel Number 941 is a message from your spirit guides that shows up to let you know that the recent boundaries you have created for yourself has allowed you to have freedom of your personal energy.

942: Angel Number 942 is a message from your spirit guides that shows up when you are called to become more selfish with your time and energy, especially with people who take more than they give.

943: Angel Number 943 is a message from your spirit guides that appears when you are being called to evolve from being a student to a teacher. There is a depth of knowledge that you have that is beneficial to others who are just beginning.

944: Angel Number 944 is a message from your spirit guides that appears when you are walking into a period of increased memories. Your dreams may be very vivid at this time and it would be best to write down whatever has been revealed to you recently and in the days to come.

945: *Angel Number 945* is a message from your spirit guides that shows up when you are going through an ego death. This is a time where spirit is calling for you to remove false perceptions of self and learn to connect with the interweb of people in the universe.

946: *Angel Number 946* is a message from your spirit guides to learn new ways to process your anxious energy when it arises. Are there any lifestyle changes you can make? Breathing exercises? What can you do that is less expensive and effective? It's time to start researching.

947: *Angel Number 947* is a message from your spirit guides that appears when you are being summoned from your hermit mode to connect with the outer world. You have recharged your energy and now it's time to get back out there, connect, and learn.

948: *Angel Number 948* is a message from your spirit guides reminding you that if you stay ready, you won't have to worry about getting ready when the time comes. Plan as if it is already here.

949: *Angel Number 949* is a message from your spirit guides reminding you that when you encounter someone with a bad attitude it is about them and has nothing to do with you. Make sure to stay grounded as they go through their motions at this time.

950: *Angel Number 950* is a message from your spirit guides to allow things to happen when they happen. It is best to not intervene with anything that is following divine order at the time. The last thing you want is to take on someone else's karma.

951: *Angel Number 951* is a message from your spirit guides calling for you to embrace your uniqueness. You were not created to be like everyone else and it is best to love what makes you different versus cry over how you're not like everyone else.

952: *Angel Number 952* is a message from your spirit guides letting you know that others see the changes you have been making and how it has changed you for the better. They are all bragging about how much you have changed and are glowing.

953: Angel Number 953 is a message from your spirit guides reminding you that it is always good to be flexible in situations as you never know what may happen or why something has to happen. Learning flexibility can be hard, but worth it when faced with challenges.

954: Angel Number 954 is a message from your spirit guides asking you to take a look around you and notice who is still in your life after a period of change. These are the people who see the good in you as they are able to accept you for all of your changes you've gone through over time.

955: Angel Number 955 is a message from your spirit guides calling for you to make sure you are not overlooking anything at this moment. Go back and cover your tracks to make sure no important details are missing from a project you are working on.

956: Angel Number 956 is a message from your spirit guides reminding you to not judge yourself for things you can not change. Even the things you can change, it's important to have compassion for yourself versus contempt.

957: Angel Number 957 is a message from your spirit guides calling for you to change your views on money and spending. This is not the time to be holding too tightly to your money as that gives the energy of lack and deficiency. When in this space it makes it harder to manifest. When you are buying something or getting a gift, do it with an open and cheerful heart and it will be returned to you tenfold.

958: Angel Number 958 is a message from your spirit guides reminding you that it is always good to give back to others who may have less than you. It's a reminder that we are all on this journey together and we all have the ability to be a blessing to someone else, which makes you feel good in return as well.

959: Angel Number 959 is a message from your spirit guides calling for you to take a step back and have a more reserved approach to life right now. The less involved or aroused you allow yourself to be, the easier it will be to get through whatever is going on.

960: Angel Number 960 is a message from your spirit guides that comes when you are coming out of a period of hermit mode and are re-emerging into society. Spirit is saying, don't be shy, it's ok to jump head first and show the world that you mean business.

961: Angel Number 961 is a message from your spirit guides that shows up when they want to make sure you do not forget who you are and how far you have come.

962: Angel Number 962 is a message from your spirit guides that shows they are giving you permission to flex a skill you have that not many others possess. Allow yourself to relish in your greatness today.

963: Angel Number 963 is a message from your spirit guides that appears when your spirit guides want you to make sure you do not allow others' perceptions of you to alter your personal actions.

964: Angel Number 964 is a message from your spirit guides to reorganize your life and personal space to fit your new schedule or home life. As your life changes, so does your schedule and needs.

965: Angel Number 965 is a message from your spirit guides to try tame your excitement and wanting for fun right now. It is best to find a balance between being structured and free in order to make the best of your life situation.

966: Angel Number 966 is a message from your spirit guides that shows up when they want you to know that you are doing an amazing job with what you have been given in this lifetime. You have been a great steward and can expect more abundance to come your way.

967: Angel Number 967 is a message from your spirit guides calling for you to clear out any energy that is not in alignment with your purpose, life callings, and professional needs. They are just distractions right now.

968: Angel Number 968 is a message from your spirit guides that shows up when they want to bring to your attention that there may be too many chefs in the kitchen trying to give orders. Even if you are the one in the leadership position, sometimes it's best to just let someone think they are right in a situation they really aren't.

969: Angel Number 969 is a message from your spirit guides when you are being called to find the perfect balance between being in hermit mode and around others. It's ok to spend a lot of time alone but you do need people in order to reach full potential.

970: Angel Number 970 is a message from your spirit guides calling for you to never stop learning new things. Your drive to learn and develop new skills is a strong characteristic trait that many do not possess.

971: Angel Number 971 is a message from your spirit guides that shows up when you are on the verge of a promotion in your work field. No matter what you do as a profession, you are getting recognized and others see how much you put into your daily work.

972: Angel Number 972 is a message from your spirit guides that appears when you have reached a particular intellectual level in your life. You didn't notice the things you are seeing now, because you weren't aware of them before.

973: Angel Number 973 is a message from your spirit guides letting you know that you have unlocked a new level in your life. You are walking into a creative period of your life that will open new doors for you, have patience with yourself as you walk through.

974: Angel Number 974 is a message from your spirit guides when they want for you to finally break away from ways of your upbringing that are no longer working for you. You may be holding on to outdated beliefs and feelings that are no longer working for you.

975: Angel Number 975 is a message that shows up from your spirit guides when you are approaching a new beginning in your life. They are calling for you to prepare for this beginning by researching and making sure your mindset is in alignment with change.

976: Angel Number 976 is a message from your spirit guides letting you know that you have a divine team working on your behalf at this time. Open your eyes to the world around you and realize anything is possible as long as you are in alignment with it.

977: Angel Number 977 is a message from your spirit guides calling for you to embrace your past as the lessons it taught you, but do not let it succumb you in your present day. Allow it to inform you, not overcome you.

978: Angel Number 978 is a message from your spirit guides that shows up when you are being called to incorporate lessons you have learned from difficult past situations into your current life. You will find that its wisdom helps you develop compassion for life and hope for the future you are creating.

979: Angel Number 979 is a message that is received from your spirit guides when they are asking for you to take the energy around you at face value. It is important to understand the messenger just as much as the message that is being shared. Look below the surface of all things and people around you to see their core.

980: Angel Number 980 is a message that shows up when you are going through a spiritual upgrade. It is imperative for you to define your needs and goals strategically and concisely because anything is possible.

981: Angel Number 981 is a message from your spirit guides that shows up when they are calling for you to learn how to embrace all sides of yourself. Even the ugly parts that you wish didn't exist. It all has a purpose.

982: Angel Number 982 is a message from your spirit guides that shows up when you are in need of learning how to balance both your dark and light energies in order to find true balance of self and your magical self. All parts of you are Divine and the sooner you embrace it, the sooner you will find resolution.

983: Angel Number 983 is a message from your spirit guides that appears when you are on the verge of reaching a manifestation that you spoke into existence. You are a divine manifester and what you speak comes into existence when you truly believe and are in alignment.

984: Angel Number 984 is a message from your spirit guides to inform you that you have a strong ancestral lineage and the blood of your ancestors are still running through your veins. If you haven't communicated with your ancestors who are on your spirit team, it is time for you to start getting closer to them.

985: Angel Number 985 is a message that shows up when you are being called to explore your personal skills and magic that has always been inside of you. Allow yourself to explore who you are and what you can do without boundaries.

986: Angel Number 986 is a message from your spirit team to stop being so uptight and strict with yourself. It is ok to release a little and let things flow as they want.

987: Angel Number 987 is a message from your spirit guides to release yourself from fear and allow yourself to fully bloom into who you are called to be. Once you release it, you will find things start to get in order on their own.

988: Angel Number 988 is a message from your spirit guides letting you know that there are people from your past looking at you with regret. They regret how they treated you and tried to outcast you. Everything you did was from a pure place and now they are realizing it.

989: Angel Number 989 is a message from your spirit guides informing you to stay alert to the energy around you at this time as there is a surprise enroute to you. Others are grateful for you and allow them to shower you when they feel called.

990: Angel Number 990 is a message from your spirit guides asking for you to have more grace for an ending that had to happen in order for you to receive an abundance of blessings and direction of your life.

991: Angel Number 991 is a message that your spirit guides send you when they feel you are ready to start something new. You have built up the confidence to not only believe in yourself but to embrace and trust the journey.

992: Angel Number 992 is a message that appears when your spirit guides are calling for you to embrace your connections with others in your life after going through a period of forgiveness. The compassion you have shown them is coming back to you multiplied when you need the same.

993: Angel Number 993 is a message from your spirit guides calling for you to embrace your hobbies more and find solace in the peace they bring you. You may have been working too much and need time to just do something with no responsibility.

994: Angel Number 994 is a message that shows up from your spirit guides when they are calling for you to travel to a new location and see how your spirit feels in that location. Learning astrocartography would be a great start to your journey of exploration.

995: Angel Number 995 is a message that shows up from your spirit guides when you are called to release any inhibitions that have been trying to keep you from experiencing what life has to completely offer you.

996: Angel Number 996 is a message from your spirit guides letting you know that your heart chakra has been opened completely and you are a strong conduit and vessel for love.

997: Angel Number 997 is a message from your spirit guides that appears when you are walking into a period of luck after losing a lot. Be hopeful and excited for what is enroute to you now.

998: Angel Number 998 is a message from your spirit guides that appears when your guides are calling for you to take more responsibility for your life and how it turns out. Make sure you aren't giving your power to anyone else. It's time to take over and make things happen.

999 Angel Number 999 is a message from your spirit guides letting you know that your crown chakra has been open and activated. You are a divine vessel and have a direct connection to the higher power and energy.

Chapter 12: Common 4-Digit Angel Numbers

1001: Angel Number 1001 appears in your life when your spirit guides want you to realize you are mirroring someone in your life right now. Always remember, everyone you come into contact with is a mirror of a part of yourself that you are called to become aware of and either heal or embrace.

1010: Angel Number 1010 appears in your life when your spirit guides want you to know you are in alignment with others who are on the same page as you. You are amongst good company who can be considered an equal to you and your vibration. A karmic cycle has been completed and you are joining with others who are on a similar path.

1111: Angel Number 1111 appears in your life when your spirit guides want you to embrace your spiritual growth and transformation at this time. It shows up to be a reminder that the journey is not linear, yet a joy when it is embraced for what it is. Allow your third eye to be opened and embrace your transformation.

1133: Angel Number 1133 appears in your life when your spirit guides want you to merge your spiritual self with your creative self in order to alter your reality. This angel number appears when you are called to pay close attention to your thoughts and perception of your ability to manifest and create the life you want.

1144: Angel Number 1144 appears in your life when your spirit guides want you to take an assessment of your life and see what is working and what is not working in order to see what needs to stay and be developed more and what needs to be ended.

1155: **Angel Number 1155** appears in your life when your spirit guides are calling for you to put into practice the lessons you have recently learned. Have you made the changes required? Have you asserted yourself when called? This is your time to make sure you are following your inner guidance with grace for yourself.

1212: **Angel Number 1212** appears when your spirit guides want you to know that you have been given divine authority and leadership over an area of your life. It is a reminder that whatever is written in the stars with your name can not be taken from you by anyone. You are ordained for this position.

1221: **Angel Number 1221** appears when you may be in a current situation that is triggering to you, especially with leadership. If you are having a hard time with someone else in your life, you are being called to change your perception to one of understanding and always remember, it has nothing to do with you; it's the energy you are feeling.

1234: **Angel Number 1234** appears in your life when your spirit guides want you to know that you are in perfect alignment with your earthly assignment at this time. They want you to get ready for a big change in your life that will push you even further; keep going!

1313: **Angel Number 1313** appears in your life when your spirit guides are letting you know that you are currently going through an ego death transformation. Parts of you and your personal perception of the world are dying in order to make room for new beginnings and perceptions that allow you to manifest more. It may not be easy now, but the sooner you surrender, the easier the process will be.

1414: **Angel Number 1414** appears in your life when your spirit guides are letting you know that it would be best to enjoy the ride you are currently on, versus fight it. Life is changing rapidly and it's all happening for your betterment. Enjoy it because things will look totally different this time next year.

1515: **Angel Number 1515** appears to you when your spirit guides are reminding you of the importance of structure and organization in your life. When you see this sequence it is letting you know that it's ok to get help from someone else if needed.

1551: Angel Number 1551 appears when your spirit guides feel you are at a period of your life when you should make sure you are surrounding yourself with people and organizations that match your inner child energy. You want to make sure you can be your complete self and not have to hide to appease anyone.

1661: Angel Number 1661 shows up when you are called to pay attention to how others in your field of work, or living the life you're working towards, handle their day to day business. When it comes to manifesting it is important to have all of the systems in place that will help you and keep you protected in the future if any problems arise. This is the time to learn from others how to do something.

1771: Angel Number 1771 is an angel number that shows up when your spirit guides want for you to take some time to join forces with someone else to figure out how to do something .This is the time to find your spirit team that can push you to higher levels intellectually and spiritually.

1881: Angel Number 1881 appears when you are being called to look in the mirror and make sure you are not only addressing the difficult parts of yourself but taking the leadership role in your life. This is a reflective time to address any areas of insecurity or lack of self-accountability.

1991: Angel Number 1991 appears when your spirit guides are calling for you to give yourself credit for how much you have changed and grown over time. As you allow yourself to reflect over the different phases of your journey, it will allow you space to have more compassion and understanding for yourself as you continue to end cycles and begin new ones.

2020: Angel Number 2020 shows up when your spirit guides want you to know you are seeing things clearly at this time. You are on track with your journey and whatever is going on around you, it has no way to hide as you are in-tune with your intuition. Continue to trust it.

2112: Angel Number 2112 shows up when your spirit guides want for you to reflect back on your childhood. There may be something you have tried to hide or cover up that needs to be addressed in order for you to completely heal a hurt or pain that you experienced as a child. No more Band-Aids, allow it to finally heal.

3003: Angel Number 3003 shows up when you are being called to allow your creativity to fly free! It will do you no justice to limit your creativity as it is an avenue of self-expression that opens more doors in your everyday lives, than you may realize.

4567: Angel Number 4567 appears when you are getting prepared for a new role in your life. You have taken the steps required to obtain the needed knowledge, order, and grace for yourself. Your hopeful and inner childlike energy has set you up for success and it is here.

I hope you were able to find what you needed in order to connect more with your intuition as the numbers and messages appear around you. For numbers not included, it is advised to use the numbers separate to find the complete message. It will be exactly what you needed to hear.

Printed in Great Britain
by Amazon